Manipulation by Guilt:

How to Avoid It

Manipulation by Guilt: How to Avoid It

by Dr. Harry E. (Bud) Gunn

Greatlakes Living Press, Ltd., Publishers,
Waukegan, Illinois

Manipulation by Guilt: How To Avoid It
© Dr. Harry E. Gunn 1978
All rights reserved
Printed in U.S.A.
International Standard Book Number: 0-915498-98-7
Library of Congress Catalog Card Number: 77-84653

Greatlakes Living Press, Ltd.
91 N. Noll Street
Waukegan, Illinois 60085

Contents

To my wife, Vi, a complete partner in all that I undertake, and to Dr. Joseph C. Rheingold, the finest teacher of psychology I have ever known

1

Introduction

If you talk to an author about the creation of his book, you will generally get the impression that hours of planning took place long before a word was written. It has been stated that many well known, learned writers spend many hours working and reworking the first sentences. Surely the entire creative process is heavily veiled in mysticism. Hours of creative thought proceed the writing of a single word.

However, such was not the case with this book: it was created by accident! Even so, the experience was nonetheless interesting. When I first had submitted my idea for publication, I was certain that my publishers would be as fascinated by my proposal as I was. In fact, they were not. Incredulous, I failed to absorb their reasons for rejection. The meeting concluded, suspending further consideration of my work.

Later my publishers told me they felt guilty about the rejection, recognizing my commitment to the book. They wondered if I would not consider another project and suggested some aspect as a general topic, of human motivation. If I would consider this, they in turn would be willing to extend the deadline for the book for as much as a month.

I was not enthralled with this new development but upon reflection, felt guilty because they had been so considerate. Publishers *were* human after all, I found. But what could I write about—human motivation was a very big, generalized topic.

That night my wife and I were invited to a friend's house for dinner. The dinner at home was arranged because the couple had cancelled out of a dinner with us at our favorite French restaurant. It seems they had felt guilty because their eight-year-old had complained that they never included him in their dinner plans. He liked to talk to adults too, he had informed his parents.

We spent most of that evening listening to him talk about all the touchdowns he had scored in his junior football league. He stayed up until 11:00 P.M. because his parents felt too guilty to send him to bed at his regular time. When he finally did go to bed, we were all exhausted from our evening of football replays. His parents were so guilt-ridden by this experience that they forced three glasses of their best wine upon my wife and myself.

The next morning I had a hangover and felt guilty because my cloudy head made it difficult for me to work. My wife, Vi, tried to encourage me but I just couldn't get moving. We talked for a while and suddenly Vi said she had to take the kids to a basketball game. "I'd feel awfully guilty if they are late!" she exclaimed.

The thought struck with a mighty blow. "You mean that you are motivated by *guilt*," I retorted. She answered in the affirmative and I proceeded to lecture her on succumbing to that "irrational" emotion. "There must be others like you," I declared. "I think I'll write a book to free all you poor slaves." And so the idea was born, and I got over my guilt about letting down my kindly publisher.

There are three primary emotions that haunt the human psyche, creating untold misery and robbing individuals of their ability to be creative as well as joyful. Two of these, depression and anxiety, are well covered in contemporary literature. The third emotion, guilt, is barely mentioned despite the fact that millions of people are afflicted by it for major portions of their lives.

Guilt as an emotion has some very handicapping qualities. It prevents people from enjoying nearly everything they do. The guilt-ridden person is unable to relax, cannot joyfully relate to others, and is blocked from the satisfaction of work well done. In addition to losing pleasure the guilt-ridden person often finds it difficult to control his actions. He feels impelled to senselessly rebel from time to time just to prove that he is a free soul. In so doing he is inclined to do things dangerously and thereby create new problems for himself. It has been said that the guilt reaction does not prevent people from doing anything—it just stops them from having fun. As a therapist I have found this clique somewhat correct, although there are many cases where people did withdraw because of their guilt reactions.

I also believe that in our society it is more important than ever before to understand the workings of the guilt mechanism. Organized advertising campaigns cause us to feel guilty when we don't purchase a particular product. We are manipulated by government and by political campaigns. There are even books telling us how to gain an advantage by manipulating others.

I am against these methods of manipulation, but I like to see people relate to each other in a constructive manner, free to say yes or no as it fits their needs. No one can perform well when they do not really want to. This is true when spending time with children, and just as true in the act of making love. We don't have to manipulate to achieve our goals; we just have to become free, loving people.

These thoughts, coupled with my professional experiences, prompted me to write this book. I think the reader may be surprised at just how widespread manipulation by guilt is. I believe that if the reader can see how manipulation by guilt works, he will be better prepared to deal with the problem. Once we are aware of the manipulation process, we must also look at ourselves to see if we are also using guilt to manipulate others.

If we can obtain a personal freedom from guilt, perhaps we'll find more creative ways of interacting and a more constructive, joyful life.

One word of clarification about this book. Confidentiality is important to the psychologist. Towards that end all names and places have been changed with the exception of those who lead exemplary, constructive lives. Some people are so helpful to their fellow humans that

they deserve all the credit they can get. Those, however who have sought help are protected by pseudo-
nyms, and if they sound familar it is only because guilt
is so widespread.

2

The Nature of Guilt

What Is Guilt?

If you were to ask a professional person to define guilt, you would probably get many different responses. Most would be highly technical and somewhat ambiguous. Putting the question to an untrained person would generally produce a uniform response. "Guilt is when you feel bad because of something you did or want to do," came back the answer over and over again.

I like the answer; it is simple and it can be put into an emotional context. When we deal with human behavior, it seems more important to talk about how people feel than how some term is defined. All of us can understand what it means to feel "bad" or "guilty," but few can understand what "super-ego conflict" feels like. Feeling as I do, therefore, it seems most pertinent to talk of how guilt makes us feel, how and why we become manipulated, and what our behavior is likely to become in the face of it.

That does not mean that I wish to completely divorce myself from technical opinions on guilt. It does mean that I don't wish to dwell upon them, either. Freud once stated that neurotic guilt is clearly noticeable in later life. As an adult a person experiences the same guilt reaction he would have as a child. To me this means that many adults are ruled by a threat to the same extent that a child is so ruled. We don't seem to grow and develop strength in this area as would be expected. We are therefore handicapped.

Let us tentatively define guilt as a feeling that we have done or felt something unacceptable to someone. When we include behavior in this definition we must note that one thing we may have done wrong is to be *inadequate*. By failing to do something in an acceptable way we feel we may have displeased someone, hence a guilt reaction. That concept broadens the scope of guilt, but it is very fitting. After all, do not many children feel guilt because they didn't do as well in school as was expected of them?

When we look at guilt in this manner we see that feelings of inadequacy can well be related to feelings of guilt. So too is dependency because in our desire to reduce guilt feelings we must try to be what others want us to be. The guilt-ridden person clings to his model or models because he must always try to justify himself. Depression, too, may be related to guilt because the guilt-ridden person, feeling inadequate, has a tendency to withdraw from personal interaction, causing feelings of loss, rejection, and loneliness. There is also a tie between guilt and anxiety that seems worthy of exploration.

Guilt Versus Anxiety

On the surface guilt and anxiety are easily distinguished. Anxiety may be defined as a type of fear wherein the source of the threat is unknown. Fear is specific, anxiety is not. With anxiety we experience a vague threat and the hidden nature of the threat makes it a different emotion with which to cope. People can generally cope with what is known, irrespective of how frightening. But when we don't know what we are threatened by, as in anxiety, we can't easily conquer the threat. It also is important to note that anxiety is "free floating," or in other words, spreads from one situation to the next.

Guilt, on the other hand, is a feeling that one has done or felt something wrong, or, of course, failed to do something that *should* have been done. There is once again a vague threat of some sort of punishment and for that reason guilt and anxiety are clearly related. I have seen over the years that those people who test high in regard to guilt feelings also show a high level of anxiety, but the reverse is not always true.

From Where Does Guilt Stem?

There has been much discussion about the source of guilt but there remains much disagreement. In his monumental book, *The Mother, Anxiety, and Death,* Dr. Joseph C. Rheingold touches on the subject of guilt in a manner that certainly jibes with what I have seen. He talks about the concept of threat. This threat results from mobilizing the mother's anger, generally by not doing something that mother wished done.

This concept is different from earlier explanations because the prior idea was that children were simply afraid (and therefore guilt-ridden) at the prospect of losing the love of the parent. I believe that both parents may produce guilt feelings in the child by a threatening attitude when the child doesn't conform. I have also noted that threat comes not solely from hostile actions but also from hostile parental feelings. A young man I saw in therapy for several years spoke about the "rage" of his parents, and he lived in dread of them well into his twenties. I felt sure that, from the intensity of his fear, his parents must have physically abused him. However, he told me one day that neither parent had ever touched him. He recognized their anger, properly called rage in this case, and feared that one day they would literally tear him apart.

This may sound unusual, but don't we often fear a person whose anger we sense even though he hasn't threatened us physically? We sense the underlying anger and fear that it will one day be acted out upon us. If we adults know this kind of fear, what must the child go through?

I believe all guilt originates from the fear a parent will harm us for what we do. This may even include our thoughts since many parents attempt to control their children's minds.

After the dynamics have been set for guilt in child-hood, anything later in life may once again set off the reaction. The guilt-ridden person becomes an easy target for everyone and everything. In addition, if guilt has been used on the child, he may identify with the approach and use it on others. It is particularly likely that he will use it on his children. In this manner, guilt becomes transferred from one generation to the next. The whole process may be unconscious, but that only makes it more difficult to detect and control. Of course, the major question is what all of these guilt feelings do to us.

The Effects of Guilt

There are some who would argue that mankind needs guilt feelings in order to monitor his so-called dangerous impulses. Advocates of this viewpoint feel that anticipation of guilt maintains a check on sexual behavior, on dishonesty, and hostile impulses. To remove guilt feelings, they argue, would be tantamount to destroying civilization.

It is true that some persons will claim that guilt deters them from a particular behavior. However, I still do not believe that guilt feelings work for the betterment of man. There are other types of controls that are more precise and do not destroy the personality in the process. In fact, I feel it is quite easy to show how guilt feelings may do just the opposite of their intent. Instead of providing a controlling factor, they cause unwarranted action. Let's look at some of the principles involved in the guilt reaction and see why.

1.) Generally speaking, the guilt-reaction takes place *after* the act has taken place. That means we may not enjoy what we did but the guilt did not deter the action. It may in the future but not indefinitely.

2.) Guilt feelings hamper personality development because people who suffer from them become fearful of any kind of activity. These people find it difficult to be normally assertive and creative. They constantly watch

themselves and in so doing lose spontaneity. They become self-centered and constantly complain about their
loss of freedom.

3.) The guilt reaction causes dependency (and vice
versa) because the afflicted person is always looking to
others for support. He wants everyone to tell him that
he isn't as bad as he thinks he is.

4.) Guilt-ridden people love to see others fail because that gives them company in feeling "bad." If
everyone else does it too, so to speak, they can't be so
bad.

5.) Guilt causes us to be easily manipulated by others because the guilt-ridden are so concerned about
what others think. Therefore, these people can easily
be led into activities over which they have conflict. In
fact, that makes it easier for them because they can
then blame the manipulator.

6.) The guilt-ridden also manipulate others through
guilt. That is the game they know best. They repeat
that which has been done to them.

7.) The guilt reaction makes it difficult for people to
joyfully give of themselves. Interaction is dulled, fraught
with anger and frustration.

8.) The guilt-ridden person suffers from his guilt feelings. He does not like the pain and will punish others
for his discomfort.

9.) Guilt-ridden people feel unworthy of receiving
anything good from other people. As a result, when
someone does something good for these people, they
often reciprocate anger, not thanks. That becomes a
most important principle, which helps explain why so
many people hurt those who do the most for them.

10.) Those who are guilt-ridden need punishment in
order to lessen their guilt feelings. Consequently, they
frequently do those things that they deem most wrong.
Then they seek punishment and for a time their account
is balanced. This means, however, periodically their
guilt acts as a stimulus to action that is contrary to
many of their values.

11.) Those who feel guilty can't stand the feelings of
helplessness that guilt produces. They don't know when
the axe is going to fall and the vagueness of the threat

is unbearable. Periodically they perpetrate the "forbidden act" to prove their valor. They act defiantly and then try to find out exactly what the threat they fear is or how severe it will be.

12.) The guilt-ridden act covertly because they fear public censure. That means they often attack others in a most secretive and destructive manner, avoiding the issues.

13.) Guilt-ridden people seek justification of their acts. Rationalizing, they may claim that morality is on their side. Their claim is a restatement of "the end justifies the means." Another rationale is that some group is so objectionable that we need special norms in dealing with them. They are outside the bounds of human limits. Hitler's approach was a notable example of this.

14.) The guilt-ridden person disavows his guilt, projects it onto others and then publicly denounces his fellow mankind. That is why the guilt-ridden town gossip so often ruthlessly attacks others for doing that which he (or she) would like to do.

As we go over these principles we can see the wastefulness of this process. Once set in motion, the guilt mechanism can resonate endlessly—occasioning guilt responses in others as well. Eventually the guilt surfaces as anger. Most of us are manipulated by others; in turn, we manipulate back. Human interaction suffers as a result, and there is a loss of joy, creativity, and self-fulfillment.

My aim in writing this book is to reduce that conflict by some small measure and to restore our just portions. To do that, we require a measure of self-awareness. It would be helpful to first understand how guilt-prone we are. Toward that end, let me invite you to take the quiz that immediately follows I believe you may find it helpful in assessing your guilt feelings.

Quiz

Instructions: Please check the following statements as to whether you agree, disagree, or are uncertain that the statement holds true for you. The answers are given immediately following the quiz.

	Agree	?	Disagree
1.) I never do things that I later regret.	☐	☐	☐
2.) I have frequent temper outbursts.	☐	☐	☐
3.) I am a very dependent person.	☐	☐	☐
4.) I am described as very easygoing.	☐	☐	☐
5.) I frequently have digestive problems.	☐	☐	☐
6.) I often make purchases that I regret later.	☐	☐	☐
7.) I am not a moody person.	☐	☐	☐
8.) I find it easier to say no than to say yes.	☐	☐	☐
9.) I have many little pleasures in life.	☐	☐	☐
10.) I enjoy being with people.	☐	☐	☐
11.) Decisions are hard for me to make.	☐	☐	☐
12.) I am not afraid of anything.	☐	☐	☐
13.) I generally feel secure and confident.	☐	☐	☐
14.) I generally sleep very well.	☐	☐	☐
15.) I never leave anything on my plate.	☐	☐	☐
16.) I don't like to see anyone with an empty glass when I give parties.	☐	☐	☐
17.) I am always helping other people.	☐	☐	☐
18.) I feel that others should make up their own minds.	☐	☐	☐
19.) Nothing ever worries me.	☐	☐	☐
20.) I am an excessive drinker.	☐	☐	☐
21.) I am terribly annoyed by the immoral behavior of others.	☐	☐	☐
22.) I want more out of life than I have now.	☐	☐	☐
23.) I like to see others grow and develop.	☐	☐	☐
24.) Most people can be trusted.	☐	☐	☐
25.) I am a completely honest person.	☐	☐	☐
26.) People always come to me with their problems.	☐	☐	☐
27.) I enjoy physical activity.	☐	☐	☐
28.) I have good sexual adjustment.	☐	☐	☐
29.) It never disturbs me to be different from others.	☐	☐	☐
30.) My parents were never satisfied with my school performance.	☐	☐	☐

Quiz Answers

1.) Disagree
2.) Disagree
3.) Disagree
4.) Agree
5.) Disagree
6.) Disagree
7.) Agree
8.) Disagree
9.) Agree
10.) Agree
11.) Disagree
12.) Disagree
13.) Agree
14.) Agree
15.) Disagree
16.) Disagree
17.) Disagree
18.) Agree
19.) Disagree
20.) Disagree

21.) Disagree
22.) Agree
23.) Agree
24.) Agree
25.) Disagree
26.) Disagree
27.) Agree
28.) Agree
29.) Disagree
30.) Disagree

All questions answered with a question mark count as two wrong answers. The question mark shows uncertainty, which is then correlated with guilt. When you have added up your incorrect answers you may rate yourself according to the scale.

Self Rating Scale - Total Numbers of Errors

0 - 6 Very guilt free

7 - 12 Some obvious areas of guilt

13 - 19 Definitely guilt-prone

20 - 25 Severe guilt tendencies

25 - 30 You are easily manipulated

30 or more: You suffer and beg others to manipulate you.

3

Our Heritage: A Society Built Upon Guilt?

The aim of this chapter is to show how we had already planted the seeds of guilt in our early beginnings. This is not meant as an indictment of society, history or the founding fathers. Certainly, they had some glorious goals and their creation was a noble experiment. One cannot sit back now and criticize because the whole world situation has changed. Our aim, then, is to understand and not to judge.

Our inquiry should naturally start with the question why people came to this country. Obviously there were many reasons, but two seem to have prevailed. One was to escape from religious and political persecution. The second was for greater financial gain. We all recognize the state of affairs that existed in the world at the time of our beginnings. There were literally religious wars all over the place. People were not free to practice their beliefs if their beliefs were contary to the group that held power. So those who were in the minority sought refuge in a land where they would be free to establish their own way of life. Naturally this was easy to do in America because those who arrived first could set up their way of life first.

One might expect that those who have known the sting of persecution would recognize the pain and not repeat the injustice. However, human beings are seldom

that rational as our early history of persecution evidenc-
es. Attack from the outside creates group solidarity and
it did just that in America. As a result there were attempts to make people of different faiths feel like out-
siders.

There is another important factor too. Persecution
can consolidate a group, so that its members are not
open to change. Differences of opinion are simply not
tolerated. The very orthodox remain strict in their views
and are not challenged by the liberals in their midst.

The main concern of those brilliant men who established our government was loss of freedom to the government, not to strong individuals. Originally they set up
many rules restricting government, but placed few restrictions upon individuals. The founding fathers were
careful to define and limit those freedoms that could not
be touched by government.

As a result we allowed whole groups of people to be
enslaved, other groups to be barred from employment
and one entire group, women, to be unable to vote and
in some cases unable to even own property. People
could be bought and sold as long as the government
didn't do it. That we even allowed certain religious beliefs to be legislated can be seen from many of our
laws on sexual behavior, child labor, and even working
on Sunday.

In the early days any arguments against the popular
faith produced a severe reaction. It is very likely that
many of our early leaders felt strong guilt reactions
when there was talk of change in moral or philosophical
values. If you read of the personal lives of these men
you will find that they often did not live by what they
preached. Yet they were not free to change their thinking. That is generally a sign of guilt. For the guilt-ridden
person, thought and values resist change while behavior changes rapidly. If one is in a powerful position guilt
simply causes them to punish others for doing what
they themselves do or wish to do. Many of the main reasons behind the founding of our country combined to
form a national ethic. Our people were here to be successful and they could not tolerate failure. We praised

anyone who went from rags to riches, we were suspicious of inherited wealth, and we scorned failure. Those who failed had to be lazy, or stupid or inherently wanting to live off others. Of course, it was true that those who failed could always escape to new land on the frontier and with industrious work become successful. There were simply no excuses for failure. That part of our ethic exists today and we look down on failures and facilitate guilt.

In order to succeed, one had to *look* successful. They were likely to be young, strong, bright, and energetic. We did not have to follow in the footsteps of our fathers as was generally true in Europe. Anyone could break away if he had the courage. As a result those who looked ugly, old, unsuccessful and lethargic were held in disfavor.

Thrift and hard work were two other national ethics. The desire to be successful and to punish failure caused early settlers to look down on those who had fun. Because life was supposed to be serious, we didn't enjoy the plays and sporting events that were common to Europe; our people worshiped hard work and success. Waste was intolerable for the same reason. Just as religious life was built on asceticism, our early ancesters built their personal lives along the same lines.

Even the family structure was guided by an economic ethic suited to its time. A family had many children, not for the love of children, but to help on the farm. Girls were considered a liability because they could not handle the physical tasks boys could. Children had basically no rights at all, they were simply laborers. Since the young consumed more than they produced, there was little reason to consult them in a family built upon economic survival. Education was geared, not to individual capabilities but to guiding boys to follow in their fathers' footsteps. Girls by that system did not need advance education.

Women served two purposes: they worked and they produced more children. Even as to the production of children there was nothing described as fun for the woman. Not even making love: that was a part of her duty as a housewife.

It seems likely that women and children soon felt guilty by their very station in life. A woman was lucky when a man picked her for marriage. That released her father from financial burden. But certainly women and children had little direct voice in decision-making.

Perhaps then our culture had an effect in making us guilt-prone. If it did, as I believe, we have lived in those shadows for a long time. Let's hope that the sunlight of wisdom and empathy for others drives away those shadows.

4
Guilt in our Personal Lives

This chapter has special significance to me for a number of reasons. In my clinical practice, I have found it very hard to get the guilt-ridden person to recognize the extent of his guilt complex. While the client may easily recognize that guilt and manipulation play a very large role in marriage, he will generally rationalize its significance. He does this by blaming his spouse or by assuming that guilt is an inevitable part of marriage. This applies to sexual relationships in general. In consequence, it is very difficult to effect therapeutic changes.

If, however, one is able to show a client that guilt plays a role in all parts of his life one can usually begin to make a dent. The person then can begin to ask himself what he does that causes either: all persons to use guilt on him, or causes him to use guilt on everyone. The marital relationship is as complex as the parent-child relationship. Social relationships as well as general personal relationships are less emotionally ladden and, therefore, can more easily be looked at objectively.

When I am able to point out to a husband, for example, that *everyone* makes him feel guilty, he is more apt to take a look at what he is doing to foster this reaction. When that happens, he has made an important beginning.

A second important point is that no one can begin to live with others until he can begin to live with himself.

Neurosis is generally felt to be a disorder of interpersonal relationships. However, I believe that guilt can be experienced even in solitude. Granted, it will show up more in conjunction with human interaction, but it still operates within the individual. He will create his own kind of hell which he will take wherever he goes.

In addition, people learn to interact with other people according to what works most easily. If causing others to feel guilty produces the desired end, then the manipulator will use guilt. Guilt as a technique becomes a means of obtaining something even though it may not bring interpersonal harmony in the long run. Many people do not, however, think of the long-term result. Instead, they unconsciously gravitate towards that which brings immediate success. It is in that manner people learn to manipulate via guilt.

Our spending habits are very frequently affected by our predisposition to guilt—and many salespeople knowingly use that. For example, how many times have you walked into a restroom at an expensive restaurant, for example, and been confronted by an attendant with his hand out. He will expect fifty cents to turn on the tap, hand you a towel, and then throw it into the receptacle. This is hardly a necessary service, but his looks are designed to produce guilt by making you feel small if you don't tip him.

This approach is widely used these days and may be linked to inflation! It becomes difficult to save money and invest it wisely if we are obliged to present an offering to everyone with their hand out. We have become a nation of sheep, it seems, where everyone is afraid of being called cheap. Not to spend money is tantamount to advertising to the world that we are financial failures. That hurts the ego, and the resultant guilt produces the spending habit that someone else wants. Did you ever stop and ask, "How successful is the person who is trying to make me feel cheap?" Generally, the man with his hand out is less well off then you are. Well-to-do men such as H. L. Hunt seldom have the need to go around asking for hand-outs and making others feel guilty when they don't tip.

I am not suggesting categorically that you should not tip the washroom attendant that I have cited as an example. If I adopted that stand, I might well find every urinal in the washrooms I visit clogged! My point is that there is no reason to be manipulated by guilt if you do not chose to avail yourself of this or any other small service.

The solution lies in recognizing the approach being used. When you allow someone to make you feel inadequate and, therefore, guilty for no reason at all, you are paying a high price to dine at the restaurant. If you can afford that, you certainly aren't cheap! I was once most annoyed at an attendant who gave me a dirty look on my first washroom visit because I gave him a quarter. So I decided not to go through that again the second time. When my turn came I asked him if he had change for a hundred dollar bill. He asked if I didn't have anything smaller, and I replied that I never bothered with small bills. A friend with me asked if he accepted American Express, saying, "No one uses cash these days." The man seemed a bit more humble. It seems worthy of mention that he might well have had a quarter from each of us had he not used his manipulative approach. In all honesty, though, I am not one who personally believes a man is providing a service by turning on a faucet.

A friend, Bill, who purchased a new car, recounted a similar story. He had always loved Oldsmobiles but had just married and felt he could not at that time afford such an expensive car. He decided to check out lesser-priced cars and had been pleased with the Chevrolet model cars he had seen that year. Naturally price was an important consideration. So he began his queries with the question of cost.

One salesman, however, began working on him as soon as he approached him. He began laying the line on my friend that he wouldn't even quote price until he knew that Bill was a bonafide Chevrolet buyer.

"What do you mean?" Bill asked, somewhat shocked.

"Well, just this," the salesman said, "there are some people who see a Chevy as just an inexpensive car. It isn't what they would *really* like to have. Maybe they feel they can't afford something better and so we are always second choice. We want people that are really committed to Chevies because they will be repeat customers.

As Bill later recalled, he was now very much on the defensive. He knew he needed a new car for business. His current Oldsmobile was badly worn and no longer gave good mileage. Unconsciously, he thought the salesman was going to *refuse* to sell him a car. I think it fair to state that he felt he didn't really belong. There are many people in this country like that. We are a very achievement-oriented society and it is easy to induce guilt because someone feels they aren't acceptable. Bill knew he would rather have an Olds and it seemed to him the salesman had read his mind.

It is a shame Bill didn't walk out of the showroom. Especially since there are hundreds of other car agencies which would have been happy to make a sale. Instead, Bill was sidetracked by the salesman's maneuver. Rather than stay within his budget, he allowed himself to buy a car with many extra options. Unconsciously, he was trying to prove to the salesman that he really was "committed" to the Chevy model. When Bill's car arrived, a week later, he received the crowning blow. At this agency it was the salesman's job to change the license plates and the man complained so bitterly that Bill said he very nearly offered to do it himself. He did recover at the last minute and said, "You know, it doesn't really sound like you enjoy your work."

His final comment was fine, but what preceded it wasn't. Bill certainly should not have let himself be manipulated in this way. Ironically, what Bill wanted was information and that is exactly what he didn't get. My own recommendation to any prospective car buyer is: Visit at least two agencies and write down quoted prices. Get a quoted price on the model that interests you and then decide on the extras you want. Get prices on options about which you are still undecided. Write *everything* down so you know what the potential cost of the car will be. Always get figures on the new car and compare it to the value of the car you may be trading in. Then, and only then, discuss trade-in value with the salesman. Don't try to figure too many things at one time; you will have inexact information and may well be confused.

For example, another friend, Joe, once told me he found one car dealer that had offered him over $150 more for his old car than anyone else offered.

"They sure give good deals," he said enthusiastically.

However, when I asked him what his new car would cost, he didn't seem to know. He replied, "That would depend on all the extras I decide upon."

"I understand, Joe," I said, "but what would each of those extras cost?"

Joe's smile disappeared and, when I next saw him, he offered his thanks. The agency that "gave good deals on old cars," was charging him over $200 more for extras. So try to get all of the information. Someone can look awfully good in one department but can suffer in other areas.

I noticed that fact once when I went from car dealer to car dealer trying to establish a price for my old car. Each appraiser would start by telling me what was wrong with my old car. Hell, I already knew that or else I wouldn't be in the market for a new one. After two of these sessions, I told the salesman I would wait in the showroom until he brought me the final figure. Eventually I sold my old car through a newspaper ad—and got a better price than any dealer's offer.

The point is the same, though. When you feel guilty, you lose some of your judgment ability. When you don't ask questions, you don't get all the facts. Remember, you can never bargain from a strong position until you have the *knowledge* to do so. Learn to ask questions, take down information, avoid impulsive decisions and back off when you feel unsure. Unless you are buying something perishable you can always postpone your purchase. And, slowness to buy may very well prompt a second offer from the salesman that will be better than the first.

Impulsive buying is one means of quick profiteering that is widely used in this country. If someone can make you feel guilty because you take a lot of their time, they can stampede you into a purchase that you may later regret. Many items on the market today sold well because of supposed shortages.

I wish I could say that I'm personally above guilt; but, in truth, I can't. It is my hope that rather than returning this book, you will profit from my failings. With that hope in mind, I want to reveal what used to be one of my vulnerabilities.

I am a person with very special likes and dislikes. My selection of clothes makes this evident. Years ago the popular men's slack style featured pleats; it was very hard to find slacks that were flat across the front. The plain style was popular in the East, but not in the Midwest, where I live.

I have never wanted to waste either a salesman's or my time in shopping. And, I can't say that buying clothes is one of my favorite activities. Consequently, when I did venture into a clothing store I wanted to determine quickly whether they had the type of slacks I prefer. However, I realized one day that I was spending far too much time shopping. Thinking about it produced an answer: salesmen were not answering my questions about the store's stock. They avoided them by bragging about what great slacks they did have. It was the "latest style," or they had, "an extremely wide selection." I realized that guilt made me waste time looking because to do otherwise might hurt their pride in their goods. I was manipulated by my guilt and usually walked out empty-handed. Some salesman even implied that I couldn't be so inflexible as to want only *one* style.

The fact is that in terms of my preferences, I *am* inflexible. Why hide it? In my entire life, I have owned only two pairs of pleated slacks. What has worked for me, therefore, is to simply say, "I am sure you have a wide selection, but do you have pleatless slacks?" I persist and no longer feel angry about wasted time. I don't care very much about the "latest style," so that argument doesn't sway me. I find that salesmen do respond to the statement: "I make my own styles," but the main difference is my recognition of what was taking place inside me. When you do that, you will find you are less easily manipulated.

I do know many people who feel guilty about not making a purchase after they have taken up a salesman's time. That is why salespeople so often hover around you as you look through their selections. The better ones will ask if they can help but they won't push. But, in any case, why should a potential customer feel guilty? The salesman is being paid so you can use his time.

There is another important factor, too. What happens if you do purchase something you later find you don't like? Does this kind of sale actually benefit anyone? In one sense there may be some gain to the salesman because, unfortunately, most people do not return products that are unsatisfactory. The gain will only be short-term, however, since it is unlikely that you will be a repeat customer. Of course, if nearly every salesman operates this way, there is nowhere else a customer can go.

There are great drawbacks, though, to the high-pressure sale. When a person feels he has made a successful buy, he feels good. He is more likely to buy again because he links "having" things with feeling better. This is particularly true with items of clothing. Many studies show that when a person feels well dressed, he gains some measure of inner confidence. Unfortunately, it is usually short-lived and the data all suggest that basic insecurity can't be cured by a new wardrobe.

I have seen a number of depressed and insecure patients who felt that they were poor decision-makers. These feelings were reinforced by unfullfilling purchases. Their depression often deepened and they were not anxious to buy more goods. I have long felt that a more constructive approach to selling would promote more sales. The individual cannot wait for the world to change. He must instead alter himself. If you work for your money, you should insist that other people do, too.

Let them become true salesmen, not manipulators.

Guilt as a means of interaction is even more common than sales through guilt. I sometimes think human interaction would halt without the use of guilt, but, fortunately, I see many mature people do, too.

However, let us look at some social situations, or forms of interaction, that are built upon guilt. I should note that some of the following anecdotes were furnished by interested friends and acquaintances.

One such story concerned Jan, a woman who was always lonely. I would probably call her the dependent type because she could never do anything on her own. She couldn't entertain herself and had no hobbies. As soon as her husband left for work she was next door trying to set up a coffee break. Jan told everyone her problems and in the process, received much sympathy. Generally, though, what she wanted was attention and company. Lacking conversational skill, she found it easier to talk about herself.

The problem was that Jan's neighbors had busy lives. Because they had hobbies, they did not need constant company. But, once Jan was in the door, they didn't know how to get rid of her. They didn't like to hurt her feelings, which were easily bruised. Jan never concealed her state-of-mind. For months she would pop in with a statement, "I'm bored, can you stand my company?" Please note this is stated as a rhetorical question. Jan did not want to be told "No!"

Jan possessed so much skill at manipulating that everyone around her felt immediate guilt. She was manipulatively obtuse whenever a neighbor said, "Oh my gosh, it's late and I need to get my shopping done. Jan wanted to be close to others because of her dependency needs, but was not really aware of the needs of other people. People find it difficult to get away from her because they feel guilty when they try.

I call Jan's type the "Social Butterfly." They hover around people but never make real contact. How do you handle this type without creating a social scene? The main approach involves never allowing the "Butterfly" to touch ground. Stop them before they intrude on your time. Realize that if you want them for company, you are probably making a commitment for at least half a day. So stop them right at the door. Have a ready excuse regarding your day's schedule. You do not need to be hostile, just firm. A statement such as, "I'd love company, Jan, but I can't, I have to get at--", and you can fill in the blank. Do not argue: arguments constitute time spent with someone and the "Butterfly" will accept even that. If the "Butterfly" tries to argue, just repeat, "I'm sorry Jan, I'm rushed."

A closely related type is the individual who talks about his problems constantly to get attention and vent tensions. This type, which I call the "Social Parrot," does not want to solve his problems; he wouldn't have anything to talk about! The "Parrot" wants sympathy and plenty of dependency but not empathy. Usually he has the same problems year after year, and never takes advice given. It is important to remember that complaining is "Parrot's" main interaction.

Just how do the "Parrots" work? What are their techniques that inspire closeness through guilt. Generally there are two ingredients. The first is that somebody mistreats them, usually a very "non-understanding spouse." The second factor is the really big guilt producer. They flatter the victim. You are the only person who is capable of understanding; you have great insights; "I always feel better after I talk with you," etc. They never realize that you probably feel worse. You have now been set up. How can you with your great skill turn down such a poor, unfortunate creature? You may even feel guilty because *you* are lucky to have a marital partner that understands you!

Okay, so you recognize the Parrot: I will bet that three of every five readers will recognize the type. What do you do? First, watch out for the "compliment." Don't get hooked. Stop the conversation before it gets going. You can be busy; you can indicate that you like to look at the bright side of life, or you can indicate the problem sounds deep and requires a therapist. (Just don't suggest me!) Sometimes it even helps to ask the "Parrot" what he is doing to solve these problems. But

watch out because you may be opening the flood
gates.

The "Ramora" or sucker fish is similar to the "Parrot" except that the former constantly ask for advice.
Generally, the flattery is the same, but the "Ramora"
listens better. The only trouble is that they never really
heed the advice. Instead they always let you know that
your advice failed. Why? Because, like the "Parrot,"
they do not want things to improve: they merely want
someone to blame for their misery. Social interaction
means releasing anger and dependency seeking. Psychiatrists term them "hostile-dependent personalities."

Watch out for the "Ramora." They will not merely
make your days unhappy; they also harm your reputation by publically maligning your advice. The "Ramora"
is skilled at eliciting sympathy and manipulating by
guilt. They always need a "fall guy" who let them
down. Because people tend to feel sorry for the "Ramora," they are easy bait. Through manipulation the
next sucker believes that he can correct the previous
injustice by offering better advice.

The "Ramora" always has you in his debt because
he is so skilled at proving that your advice was bad.
Meaning well, you want to make it up to him. After a
time it becomes difficult to determine who is dependent
upon whom. The "Ramora" is dependent upon the victim for release of his anger while the victim becomes
dependent in another way. He keeps trying to prove his
value as an advice giver. The victim will never win.

How do we handle the "Ramora?" As long as you
fall into his trap, you can't. I once had one of these individuals in therapy and I felt it worthwhile to trap him
with his own game. He had repeatedly asked for advice, saying that "I know you have information on how
to handle people. You could tell me how to become a
better salesman but you won't!"

"All right," I said, much to his surprise. "I will give
you advice, and, since you claim I have valuable information we will assume that it will work. If it *doesn't*
we can then talk about what *you* did to mess it up."

Obviously the man had trapped himself. If the new
approach worked it was because my "good advice"

worked. It was by his definition that it was good: he said I was a great authority—I didn't. If it failed, that was his fault since he had previously claimed that my advice would be sound. In either case we could then talk about his behavior and I won either way.

In reality, I felt any advice that constituted a change of behavior would fail with this patient. He was a very angry man and sooner or later he would have to take a look at his anger. That was what isolated him from people. He had a knack of saying "hello" that made people angry.

For a time the advice seemed to be working. I tried to focus on how artificial behaviorial change had subdued his anger. I was not eminently successful: he felt that a magical change had taken place. Only after he experienced resounding defeat was he able to take a good look at his voluminous inner rage. At this point, we made significant therapeutic gains.

From the description of the "Ramora" you can see the problems they pose. As long as they make you feel guilty they can easily manipulate you into giving them more advice. You are likely to think you have failed them, believing the victim will struggle to do better next time. Don't fall into this trap. If you must give advice, (and I caution against this), pay attention to how they use it. Giving major advice is dangerous: it fosters dependency and guilt in the "adviser." So, anyone who misuses your advice should not receive more. If you have been trapped, tell the person you don't want to mislead him again.

If you really want to help, allow others to make their own decisions. People need to learn to take responsibility for their own actions. That is a property of maturity. If asked, you can provide factual information, but let the other person draw his own conclusions. After all, people need to learn to do their own thinking!

The "Social Bee" is another type of personality that you are likely to encounter. He flutters from person to person making very hostile remarks, usually in the form of humor. The "Bee" enjoys being the center of attention and usually has a well-developed wit. He doesn't care who he hurts or how badly, but he always presents himself as a humorous individual. A frustrated entertainer, he interacts through hostility. He uses guilt to manipulate when a "casualty" complains. A this point, he says, "Oh come on guy, where is your sense of humor?" The victim then becomes defensive for two reasons: he feels guilty for not laughing and for being hurt. After all, our society does not graciously accept injury to the ego. We are expected to be strong, tough, and imperious.

If you accept those ground rules, you will constantly come up a loser. You may therefore decide that when the "Bee" attacks you the best thing to do is to give it right back. If he hurts you, so this theory goes, you will hurt him. On paper it sounds good but in practice it makes you an even bigger loser. Remember, what the "Bee" wants first of all is attention and secondly a release for his hostility. He isn't looking for fun in the usual sense: pleasant, cooperative interaction makes him feel uncomfortable. He is a person who can't stand intimacy because it makes him feel worthless. He senses his own hostility and the guilt makes closeness intolerable. Consequently he drives people away.

I have a number of suggestions for handling the "Social Bee." If you are a thoughtful, constructive person you like other people who are the same. Fun is always, to healthy people more rewarding than anger. If you are, therefore, spending time with "Social Bees" and you would rather not, ask yourself why. Is it because they have made you angry? Do you feel guilty around them because of your own anger? Do you feel guilty because you would like to be away from them? If so, console yourself and remember: you are a person and you don't owe anyone anything unless your needs are met, too. Avoid "Social Bees" whenever possible. You need not run away; simply don't bother to include them in your plans.

"Oh, sure," you might reply, "but what if I *can't* get away from them?" Maybe they are friends of other people you do enjoy. In that case, you can refuse to play their game; never carry on the sparring match that the

"Bee" loves. Make direct statements such as, "My God, Jack I've never heard you say something nice about people." The trick is to say it with humor. The "Bee" will get the message. If he retorts, you can always say, "Hey guy, can't you take a little humor?"

There is another social type that you should be prepared to handle, especially in pop psychology circles. Perhaps, because of our fascination with popular psychology, it has become fashionable lately to talk more openly about feelings and problems. An offshoot of this is the popular belief that people should remove their defenses and tell all.

Recently I counselled Mary, a very pleasant woman, who reported experiencing more guilt and depressive feelings than ever before. At thirty-seven, she had never known severe emotional stress until recently. Then the family had moved to a suburb and had settled into an apartment complex. The people seemed very friendly: they were met by a "Welcome Wagon," and were immediately invited to numerous parties. Mary was surprised at how open everyone was.

There were a number of people in this group who were "great listeners," she found. Although both Mary and her husband had always been somewhat shy, they now found that their private lives and inner feelings were of interest to another couple who bombarded them with dozens of personal questions.

At first Mary and Jim avoided the questions. This was hard to do; the other couple always pressed them for answers. As a result, Jim and Mary felt guilty because they wouldn't share "themselves." Mary, in particular, had always been somewhat guilt-prone, especially in situations where she felt socially excluded. Exploring this, I found that she had *always* been acutely aware of her shyness. The vulnerability stemmed from her teenage years when she had felt excluded from her peer group for a time.

Gradually, Mary had yielded to pressure. Pushed by guilt and manipulated by others, she talked at length about private matters. For a time, this worked fine. In turn, Mary became increasingly unguarded. She made statements which she felt guilty about later. Guilt caused her to justify her position and feelings after the fact.

With increasing regularity Mary found that others in the social group would quote back to her things that she said. Often they would make comments that indicated her feelings were not acceptable. More than once she heard someone say with shock, "Oh, Mary why would you ever feel that way—that's crazy!" Naturally she felt even guiltier; since she was afraid to express all of her feelings, she became depressed.

An old joke in the field of psychology illustrates this situation well. A therapist coaxes his patient to confide some of his deeply private feelings and actions. As trust is established, the patient finally reveals some actions for which he feels much remorse.

At that point the therapist says, "My God, you did *that* !"

While clearly not realistic, this anecdote shows the worst of all approaches. It is similar to the therapist who treats a depressed man saying, "I don't know what I am going to do," by replying "I don't either."

You can't be an effective therapist if you aren't able to accept the feelings of others. Not everyone can do that. My strong conviction is we should only share deep feelings with someone who can accept and handle them. I would caution you to be careful about revealing your innermost feelings to just anyone. To become a therapist requires much training in the understanding of another's feelings; talking to novices can be harmful.

It goes without saying that people shouldn't feel guilty because they don't open up to everyone. Adults do need psychological defenses but those defenses should be realistically used. In other words, don't drop your defenses with people who can't handle what you tell them. If you feel depressed, angry, anxious, or guilty after such a conversation, don't repeat the mistake. Don't allow yourself to be manipulated by guilt because you don't make everyone a confidant. Sure, you may deprive someone else of his drive to feel powerful, but you will preserve your own indentity and comfort.

Specifically, how do you handle the pushy questioner? When he asks probing questions tell him you will have to think about it. Ask *him* if he wants to talk about his feelings. Or you can say that you share your feelings with your spouse. You may even want to tease him and say you are afraid he will send you a bill. If he persists, tell him you only speak to professionals.

Manipulation can also be effected by the professional martyr, another personality type. Years ago, I met Marsha, a middle-aged woman who complained about her over bearing mother. The mother purchased furniture for Marsha's home. After presenting them with a gift, she would visit her daughter and son-in-law's home. On those occasions when they refused her she reminded them of her contributions to their household.

I asked Marsha why she let her mother make these purchases.

"Oh, I couldn't say no, Doctor," she said. "Mother has always enjoyed doing that. She would feel useless without it."

I suggested a modified approach—a three-way conversation with mother, husband, and herself. This approach would include telling her mother that the gifts were appreciated but asking if she really enjoyed giving these items. If her mother were to say no, Marsha should have put a stop to it. If she were to say yes (as she did) then I suggested that Marsha spell out that as long as gift-giving made *mother* happy, they would be glad to accept what was offered. But these items were not to be used as bargaining units. Marsha and her husband needed the freedom to live their own lives.

Initiating the discussion was probably hardest for Marsha. To her surprise, her mother accepted Marsha's ultimatum and lived by the decision. As a result the three were able to get along well. The guilt was reduced and the hostilities lessoned. The mother did not feel "used," and the daughter and son-in-law no longer felt manipulated and guilt-ridden. My basic point here is that we should never allow people to do things for us that they really don't want to do. The martyr personality never gives for the joy of giving. (They never give anything without strings.) They use guilt to manipulate for another end. So stop them right at the beginning: if they don't give until it hurts, they can't hurt you.

I also consider loaning things to others a very dangerous practice; there are too many people who are skilled at making others feel guilty when they are refused their goods. I think it's important to learn to say no in order to avoid feeling hurt, angry, and resentful. As a lender, you are apt to feel guilty and angry when your object isn't returned. You can always indicate that you need the item or that you are "short" yourself (in the case of money).

I had one patient, Sam, who usually couldn't refuse any loan request that came his way. A man named Joe, in particular, had a knack of making him feel guilty. After a while, I realized that we had to do something to solve Sam's problem right away; talking about it just wasn't sufficient.

"Okay Sam," I said, "I want you to do something for me. The next time Joe asks to borrow something, I want you to ask for something of approximately equal value and usefulness. Then keep the item for the same period of time that Joe keeps yours."

"But what would I do with it?" Sam asked.

"Either use it or store it away. I don't care which. Just remember to keep it for the duration of your loan."

After arguing a little, Sam decided in the end to give this program a try. I saw him several weeks later and he had a big smile on his face as he entered my office. He laughingly said, "You know, Doctor, these last two weeks have been fun. Joe needed his tool set to fix my lawn mower that he had borrowed. My lawn had been mowed so I decided to let *him* wait. He offered to help me fix what I was supposedly working on. So I had to find a project. Fortunately, my wife suggested a leaky kitchen sink. We worked all Saturday morning and then it rained. Sunday morning Joe returned my lawn mower; I think he is cured. I hated to give back the tool kit, though."

For just a moment, I was afraid I had created a monster. Would Sam now turn into a borrower? I looked around the office just to be sure he hadn't seen my tool kit in the corner.

"Are *you* cured, though, Sam?" I asked.

"Well, I think I see the point. Other people don't like

to loan things and they get mad when they feel manipulated to do so. Maybe that was the reason I felt angry so much of the time. I guess I do need to learn to express what I feel at the right time."

The little exercise brought about many significant changes in Sam's life. He finally realized that he was asking to be manipulated because of his passive, guilt-ridden approach to people. Eventually Sam was able to say no to people. To his gratification people began to respect him more. They also enjoyed being with him because he wasn't always so angry.

I can think of many social situations where guilt effectively prevents people from acting on their true feelings. The case of Nancy G. certainly illustrates this. Nancy, a young working woman, liked to read, to do things by herself and to enjoy late night suppers with her husband, Keith. Keith, like Nancy, was an independent type who enjoyed solitary pursuits. Both were happy with this arrangement. Unfortunately, Nancy often encountered situations where she could be manipulated by guilt.

On evenings that Nancy had planned to spend alone reading, she was besieged with invitations from well-meaning friends. They couldn't allow her to be alone because "they knew that wasn't any fun." Nancy would argue but without much success. She even found herself in this awkward situation on evenings she had planned to spend alone with Keith! Her friends respected her wishes only on evenings when she and her husband had definite plans that could not include others. As a consequence, Nancy lost virtually all of her privacy and pleasurable solitude.

Fortunately, Nancy was open to suggestion. I advised that she learn four new words: "Thanks, but I'm busy." She could always add: "Maybe we'll make it next time." As this story illustrates, it's not always easy to do your own thing—but you do have the right to choose.

Some people think it is difficult to say no. And I agree, but it is even more difficult to say yes if manipulated by guilt. Any positive action causes one to feel that they must take responsibility for their actions. They

have declared this to be fun and it is often guilt producing to have fun.

I wonder how many people have avoided seeing a
play or TV program because a critic said it was "too
sexy" or "in bad taste." The muddled question of violence on television is related to this. It has not been
clearly established that violence on TV causes a behavior modification in adults. If it did, why wouldn't the reverse be true? Do shows about "brotherly love" stop
wars? I don't think history shows that.

However, the real point is that when we have censor-
ship by critics we are leaving decisions to them. This is
tantamount to saying that we are all children who require others to decide what is good for us. What qualifications does a critic have? The next time you let one
make up your mind ask yourself that question. Who is
he? Pick what you like and then make your own decisions. You are the best judge of what you should like.

There is one final social situation that needs some
exploration. That is the one that involves the giving of
compliments or flattery. A personal example might help
clarify the situation.

Mary Ann was a very insecure girl, as anyone who
spent ten minutes around her would attest. She had
two ploys that generally attracted attention. One was
that she would constantly talk about how bad her hair,
legs, bust, eyes, figure, or clothes looked. If someone
said, "Mary Ann, I really like your dress," she would
retort, "Well, thanks, but, of course, it's all wrong for
my figure."

I once jokingly said to a mutual friend that there was
only one way to greet Mary Ann. You had to say,
"Mary Ann, I just *love* your hair, eyes, mouth, teeth,
figure, legs and dress."

"Sure," the friend replied, "and then she would say
"What's wrong with my personality?"

I feel sure he was correct, and I was not about to
occasion a lawsuit by telling her. There were obviously
problems with Mary Ann's personality and it got to the
point where people hated to be around her. People do
not like to be forced to give compliments, yet out of
guilt most were. Conversations were one-sided and

most tiring. The guilt reactions caused discomfort and that doesn't work for smooth social contact. Add to this the arguments and their reasons why Mary Ann was increasingly shunned.

I said earlier that Mary Ann had two ploys. Certainly one would have been more than enough but she came handily prepared. Her second maneuver was to corner some poor husband and begin to compliment his wife. She would lay it on thick and he, not realizing the trap, would go along. At which time Mary Ann would say, "I really admire her, I wish I had her figure," or whatever. In this way, Mary Ann would extort compliments from both the man and his wife.

The Mary Anns are perplexing individuals. Everyone seems to sense that they are basically insecure people who are easily hurt. They seem defenseless and on the surface it would appear they ask very little. Of course the trouble is they ask over and over again. They are insatiable. Yet the Mary Anns never do anything that is clearly and overtly hostile. How then do we deal with a pitiful creature who can so readily be hurt with confrontation? We must always remember that, when hurt, the Mary Anns cause even more guilt reactions in their victims and by so doing they hope to receive even more attention.

No one can ever begin to deal with a problem until they face an important question. What does that person or situation do to them?

As we talk about a variety of approaches the reader must answer for himself how he feels around a Mary Ann. I can and will tell you about my reaction. Each individual must, however, look at himself. Perhaps the reader does not mind the game-playing of giving out what are, in reality, false compliments. In that case I would suggest that you use humor, keep the compliments to a minimum, and recognize that you will have many interactions with the Mary Anns of the world. They may flock to your doorstep. Some men enjoy that type of attention. If such is the case with the reader, the problem is minimal. He may even wish to jokingly say something like, "I only give three compliments per person per evening." If firmly stated this may for a time be accepted. I do feel that there will be an increasing push for more and your firmness will be well tested.

There are people, on the other hand, who do not enjoy the type of interaction one generally has with the Mary Anns. I am one of these people, and it was helpful for me to recognize this fact. I absolutely abhor being insincere, and that is exactly how I would feel were I to give compliments when I don't truthfully feel them. Forced dependency is also unpleasant to me.

I had some experiences with the Mary Ann type in therapy and I found that I had to immediately deal with their approach to people. The very first such person said on a number of occasions, "I'll bet you don't feel that I really think well of myself."

Without much forethought I replied, "Why do you feel that way?"

The patient then went into the reasons and began to see she was *not* a very secure person. With great speed her insight allowed her to change her behavior. She found that she never received positive attention (praise) from her father. She learned to get his attention only through negativism. If she said she was a failure he would minimize her failure.

"What do you want to become?" I asked later.

"I want to be secure, confident, and independent," she answered.

"Very worthy goals," I reassured her and so we set upon a program to get her there. I supported the assertiveness of her individuality, and I have used that approach ever since. I simply reply to the Mary Anns that I am sure they know they look well, they aren't dependent upon me for their self-confidence. I set up a model for them to follow when they talk with me. I offer support but not to an extreme as far as compliments are concerned. If they ask for comparisons with other women (or men) I simply point out that I do not compare people. I accept each person as an individual and that they are not dependent upon me. If they push I persist, always with the central theme that their self-concept is not dependent upon my response. I find they actually prefer this model because it builds upon their inner strength. After all, it isn't fun having to constantly manipulate others to gain a measure of attention. When they see that their ploy doesn't work they simply cease. That way I find them more enjoyable and they receive some positive attention.

Quiz

1. **It is easy to handle praise given to us by another.**
   True   False
2. **It is helpful to generously give advice to others.**
   True   False
3. **Doing for others can be very dangerous.**
   True   False
4. **Using counter hostility is a sure way to drive people away.**
   True   False
5. **Complimenting people can be dangerous.**
   True   False
6. **It is not always beneficial to talk about your problems.**
   True   False
7. **Closeness can be dangerous.**
   True   False

8. **Psychological defenses should not be used by adults because they prevent closeness.**
   True   False
9. **Accepting guilt will ruin a relationship.**
   True   False
10. **One should generally not feel obliged to give more than they want to give.**
    True   False
11. **Those who manipulate are themselves easy to manipulate.**
    True   False
12. **If we could just show others how they are manipulating through guilt they would very likely stop it.**
    True   False

Self Exercises

1. Think of two occasions wherein you were manipulated by guilt in the purchase of some product. What could you do to change the situation?
2. Have you been manipulated by people in social situations? Try to think of three instances and what you might have done differently.
3. Can you list three things people do that cause you to feel guilt.

Quiz Answers

1. False—Being human, we need praise and our need can be exploited if we aren't careful. The more insecure we are the easier it becomes to manipulate us. Praise tends to cause people to let down their defenses and that is good only if what follows is constructive.
2. False—Too much advice fosters dependency. Instead, help others make their own decisions.
3. True—It *can* be dangerous but is not always dangerous. Never allow yourself to give more than *you* really want to give and don't give with strings attached.
4. False—Some people love hostile interaction. It is, after all, attention, and it may give them the reason they need to justify their own anger.
5. True—If insincere and overdone it is manipulation for some other goal. If truthful it is most constructive and in professional circles is called "support."
6. True—You need an empathetic listener, not someone who punishes you. You also do not want to take advantage of others. Mutual sharing is a good concept to try to achieve.
7. True—Yes, but if it is constructive it is worth the risk. We are more vulnerable in a close relationship but the big joy of life can come only through closeness with others. It is always important to realize, however, that you need not be close with everyone.
8. False—They need to be used when and where the situation demands it. Selective use is what brings appropriate interaction.
9. False—It won't hurt if gifts are given without psychological strings having been attached.

10. True—There are times, especially with children, where this may be necessary, but as a rule give quality, not quantity. Otherwise, you hurt everyone involved because of the guilt and anger that goes with the guilt of unwanted giving.
11. True—Absolutely—those who live by the sword die by the sword is a true axiom. Unwarranted manipulation shows a weakness and it is easy to turn that manipulation around. Manipulators do not have flexibility and where you can predict you can control.
12. False—We need to demonstrate that their manipulation will no longer work.

5

Advertising Campaigns: Organized Mobilization of Guilt

The other day I came home to find my children, as usual, in front of the television set. I was not even greeted with a friendly, "Hi, Dad," but received only a grunt when I said hello to them. They were too occupied to even acknowledge that the wage earner was home: the one who paid the bills so they could watch TV.

I became the center of their attention shortly, however, but not because of anything I did—no, that blasted TV set was still controlling our lives! The commercial was on and the boys wanted me to see what was being said about feeding our cat. The ploy was that in order for cats to be happy they had to have "sparkling eyes and shiny coats." I wondered about the logic of all this. Had some psychologist talked to cats and isolated that which makes them happy? We weren't sure what made humans happy or even what happiness is for that matter.

According to the announcer, though, only *their* cat food produced the desired utopia. My boys felt guilty because we were using some other cat food. Poor Tiffany, they sympathized, her coat doesn't look all that shiny. I was spared further discussion as they sought out the cat to inspect her eyes and fur. Before they cornered her, however, all was saved because the cartoon came on again and they returned to watch it. They did make a parting comment that we will need to buy that product because "we don't want Tiffany to be unhappy."

I couldn't stand the irony of the situation: to work all day long trying to alleviate people's feelings of guilt only to be defeated in my own house by a stranger. A guy on the tube with whom I can't even argue is telling my kids what to buy. It makes me want to write for equal time, but I would have to run for political office to get it. Then it would be just my luck to get elected and have my life ruined.

When the program ended I decided to talk to the boys about advertising in general. I could not let them win the war in our family without at least a counter-offensive of my own. Fortunately, all of our family members communicate well and we all sat down to talk about what had just taken place. I explained how the announcer was paid to try to get people to buy the products that sponsored his program. He used whatever technique the advertiser felt would work. He was an announcer for a child's program and he read a commercial that was designed to make children feel that they had failed their beloved cat. This would make them feel guilty and both boys acknowledged that it had done that.

I was delighted that they recognized their feelings and pointed out that the commercial had therefore worked, up to a point. The boys felt they had "let Tiffany down." The first question was: were they going to force Tiffany to eat something she didn't like? Secondly, if she did like this particular brand of cat food, were they willing to check her daily to see that there was indeed a change in her eyes and coat? They were against the first and willing to do the latter.

That was fine with me because we were now going to empirically test a product. One should always be open to new ideas but our choices should not be affected by guilt reactions.

As it turned out Tiffany did not like the new cat food; we never found out if it would affect her eyes and fur. Because we never forced our boys to eat food they didn't like, they treated their cat in a similar way.

The experience turned into a very useful one: from that time on our boys became a little more skeptical of what was said on television.

There is obviously a great dilemma for all families in the wake of experiences such as this. As parents we wish to rear our children to be truthful and to trust others. Yet we all recognize that this is not a world built entirely upon trust. We generally place our trust in newspapers and television commentators to keep us informed. In our complex, modern society this is the only way in which we can keep informed to make intelligent decisions. Children see us watching newscasters and forming opinions. It is quite natural that they will do the same.

It is apparent that we have to strike some sort of balance. We can't believe everything we hear but we also can't go to the opposite extreme and disbelieve everything. I am immediately turned off by a commercial that blatantly tries to ellicit guilt feelings. Sometimes, though the message is subtle and we miss it. Perhaps the answer lies in reducing our tendencies to feel and be motivated by guilt. When that happens the advertisers will be forced to change their approach.

Data suggests that guilt approaches work very well. For example, a study conducted several years ago proved women would not use instant products, such as tea. Further study revealed that they felt guilty because less work was involved. Less work made these housewives think of themselves as lazy.

There was an opportunity for the advertisers to provide a real service toward their customers. They could have re-educated these women to remove their guilt feelings. After all, what pride of accomplishment can be derived from needless work. It was decided, however, that an educational program was too troublesome: it was easier to reassign the wives' guilt. They sold their product by convincing these wives that they were neglecting their husbands by taking time away to make tea and coffee the old way.

The women were twice manipulated: first into buying the instant product and secondly by being pushed to spend additional time with their husbands. Who knows, maybe that precipitated more marital conflict by forcing people to interact when they didn't feel like it. One should not give something when they don't feel like giving it. That produces quantity at the expense of quality.

Several years ago a young couple approached me

for marital counseling. They reported that they had felt a growing distance in their marriage, but had no idea as to the cause. I asked them to give me some background to their marriage so that perhaps we might begin to pinpoint any undesirable changes.

From what they provided I could tell that they had many things in common, were still very much in love, and they seemed to have generally the same types of goals. Everything indicated that they had compatible personalities. Their lifestyles were characterized by spontaneity, casualness, and activity. They shared several sports, enjoyed dancing, dining out, and liked giving parties. Adding up the score one was forced to the conclusion they should be ideally suited. Yet something was wrong.

Irene gave me a clue when she said, "I know I must be failing somewhere, Doctor, and yet I have tried even harder in the last year to please my husband."

I attached great significance to this remark because Irene had given indication that something had changed. Neither of the two knew *when* a change had taken place, but whatever the change was it had not been to their liking.

"Irene," I began gently, "Can you tell me how you have tried even harder to please Bill?"

"Well, let me see—I guess with my appearance. I wanted to make him proud of me."

"And what made you feel that Bill was not pleased with your appearance?" Bill started to say something but I gestured him back into silence.

Irene's answer took some time to develop. As she explored their interaction over the past few years she began to realize that Bill had consistently complimented her on her appearance. She had recalled feeling a little uncertain of herself on her thirty-second birthday. Then she began to recall a series of TV advertisements that were aimed at woman over thirty. As she spoke, her memory of these commericials sharpened. The theme was that a woman should not let her husband down by "looking old beyond her years." "Make your man proud to be with you," she recalled the ad stating. It had all of a sudden struck her that perhaps she was not any longer the "sort of woman a man runs home home to."

Irene smiled as she stated, "I began to feel guilty because I thought that maybe Bill could no longer be proud of me."

So Irene had literally run out to purchase all of the face creams that, according to the commericials would restore her youth. It finally turned out that the spontaneity of their relationship was damaged. At night their love making played second fiddle to a variety of face creams, and yet more creams had to be applied in the morning. These facial treatments did not actually require lengthy time, but they came at inopportune moments.

The facials were only one part of the story. Irene realized that as a result of her susceptibility to television advertisements she had also changed her hair style. Previously she had worn her soft blond hair in a very natural short style. When she saw commercials she began to feel that Bill would be more attracted to her if she let her hair grow long and utilized the hair sprays that were being pushed on TV.

All told, Irene had redone her appearance because she had been made to feel guilty. She was a somewhat insecure woman prone to guilt feelings. The commercials had hit home and a product was sold. No real damage was done to Irene's appearance but the marriage was temporarily handicapped because spontaneous action was lost. Bill unconsciously became annoyed because of the delays that he experienced and because Irene seemed more self-centered. He felt she had lost some interest in him and tended to withdraw. As he pulled away Irene felt that he had lost interest in her.

One might raise serious question as to whether seemingly silly things like this would be likely to cause divorce. The answer is generally no—at least not with a couple as compatible as Bill and Irene. Any one who does marital counseling however, is struck by the fact that little things do cause an awful lot of trouble: people adjust to big problems. However, when guilt feelings take over, any relationship is bound to suffer.

I have noted in recent years that more and more advertising is so constructed that it will produce a guilt reaction. There has been recognition of the fact that unconscious motivation produces the quickest result. Advertising space, be it on television, radio, magazines, or newspapers, is costly. That means the advertisers must capture the individual's attention in literally a matter of seconds. If a person finds the ad uninteresting he will cease to pay attention and the message is lost. Most of us have been so bombarded with commercials since the advent of television that we have become bored and may ignore the message.

In one sense we can be immune from the coercion, on a conscious, rational level. But, guilt primarily centers upon the unconscious and thereby circumvents the more logical of our thinking apparatus. Let me illustrate with two vastly different kinds of approaches.

My goal is to sell Brand A deodorant and I must therefore convince you that it is the best on the market. I may claim that it has a brand new chemical that outperforms anything ever before on the market. I may go on to explain what the chemical is and how it works, but I will have to overcome copious resistance because you will say to yourself, "I have heard that one before." After all, there are only so many startlingly new discoveries per year. I might ask you to look at the label on Brand A in the stores and note that the contents are different from the other deodorants. But I better hope (1) that you understand chemistry and (2) that the contents really are different. In any case I have challenged your intelligence and I had better really have something!

Contrast this with my second approach: "Who wants to offend their friends?" If you are a modern, active man, you run the risk of underarm odor — an odor that could make it unpleasant for those who find themselves near you. Brand A will take away the fear of closeness; it will allow you to relax and be yourself."

This approach immediately provokes our guilt feelings. No one today will admit that they are not active. That has gone out of style. We accept without challenge the initial statement that activity breeds odor. In fact, unconsciously we welcome the thought of odor because that proves we are active people. Now we have to get rid of the odor, even though we see it as a badge of aggressiveness. Our fear of being offensive exists for only a moment because Brand A deodorant is going to stop the smell. Great; we now have the best of both worlds. Our reason never gets a chance to assert itself, and therefore we don't challenge the commercial.

A national propensity for guilt was well illustrated to me by a sign that I used to notice along one of our busy highways. The purpose of the billboard was to promote sales of an expensive liquor. "Relax," it proclaimed in bold letters, "you have *earned* it." That meant that if one did not drink that liquor they had not earned the *right* to do so. They were, therefore, bums; they didn't work and had not earned the right to relax. The ad never indicated that if one did not work he would not have been able to purchase the liquor. Of course the question exists, too, as to *how* hard one might have to work in order to be able to relax. Supposing someone works hard and still does not have the money necessary to buy luxury items like liquor? It is very likely that such an individual will be made to feel guilty. He has not measured up to the yardstick of success as applied by the advertisement. In that case he may turn to guilt as a means of dealing with his frustrations. What seems particularly obnoxious about the approach is that we allow someone else to dictate when and under what circumstances we will relax. Most psychologists would insist that relaxation goes along with success. The happy, relaxed individual is better able to utilize his abilities.

Another form of advertising currently in vogue hits at our image of ourselves as successful people. Americans are achievement-oriented. We like to think of ourselves as thrifty and ambitious. Those who create advertising campaigns know this. They therefore bombard us with the thought that if we are industrious and thrifty we will take advantage of bargains.

Consequently we are besieged with the message that there is a limited supply of some commodity. We must hurry or we will miss out on something of great value.

Many people are stampeded into purchases they would never make if they used their rational minds. But who among us wants to believe that he can't make quick decisions that will save money? So we buy quickly to get in on the bargain. Guilt makes us thoughtless—and shortly after our purchase what do we hear? Usually that the offer has been extended due to "popular demand."

Anyone who watches television soon becomes very aware of the commercial value of holidays. I am not even considering Christmas in this grouping because we are all painfully aware of the enormous advertising push that goes on then.

But who ever heard of Sweetest Day or National Secretaries Day before television? When the ad programs hit most of the people, out of a feeling of guilt, they feel an urgency to buy something for their secretaries or "sweetest one." Naturally the ads even tell people what to buy: they create a need for an often unneeded product. Holidays are invented to create a new market.

Guilt feelings have caused people to feel that they must conform. How many times have you heard someone say, "What I did was wrong but everyone else does it, too?" This is because guilt feelings generally stem from the deep inner impression that someone else will not like us as we are. "I have to please that person, not myself," goes that little inward voice. Consequently, an ad can succeed if it convinces the individual that everyone else is doing something. No matter what everyone else is doing is destructive; we follow without critical appraisal because our guilt tendencies take over. We never seem able to say "So what, I don't want to," (or conversly, "They aren't and I do want to").

As a result an advertiser can tell you what kind of boss you should be. Guilt-ridden people will never question it, at least as long as the message coincides with prior guilt feelings. It would be difficult to make a male boss feel guilty because he doesn't talk to his secretary or because he is not interested in her feelings. Up to now, men have not been taught to freely express their compassionate feelings: that reaks of the unmasculine. But men are supposed to be achievers and as such they are expected to bestow some of their worldly goods upon others. There is guilt when you do not live up to the image that has been created for you.

It is interesting how this pattern works. I have seen two men feel guilty because they were slow to fill out a questionaire that they hated. This was because the sender enclosed a dime ahead of time for "appreciation of their time." Yet these same men did not feel guilty for taking time away from their children. What is so strange is that neither of these men would have accepted a direct arrangement whereby they were paid ten cents for about ten minutes of work. Think of it, that comes to sixty cents an hour!

How, then, did this scheme work? By prepaying for the form to be filled out the advertiser subtly tells the victim that he has faith in him. A dime is too small an amount to be returned. To keep it is to say that the blind faith was badly placed. The advertiser thought the victim would be honest, but he turns out to be dishonest. Seemingly, something is offered for nothing, i.e., ten cents against the "risk" that the form will be thrown out. To fail to fill it out would be to let the sender down. And all of this after he had "so much faith in your honesty!"

Next time you receive a form in the mail notice how disarming the wording is. The writer tells you that it will only take you a few minutes to fill out the form." He doesn't tell you that your time is worth something. He certainly won't tell you that you, of all people, should have the right to determine how your time will be spent. For absolutely certain he won't tell you that in some manner he will make money on your free donation of *your* time.

As a psychologist I receive many of these forms weekly. Often they come from someone wanting to get my reaction to some product that will eventually be offered to the public. In essence they are asking for a free consultation. I once added up the required time for a week of filling out these forms. It came to well over an hour! I concluded that the hour could better be spent with my family. These forms were thrown out and I felt sure that in the future they would not come in such abundance. I was partially correct. There were fewer demands upon my time but a number of advertisers noted that in the past they had not received my form. I had let them down. Knowing that I was "a very busy professional and probably overlooked the questionaire" they were giving me a second chance. My waste basket is still filled at week's end but I do see some drop off of this sucker mail. I think the message is gradually getting across to the computers that tabulate who bites and who doesn't. Who knows, maybe one day I will come home and find that my mail consists only of bills.

What is the effect of all of this commercial mobilization of guilt? Is it good for the individual, the consumer, the producer, and even the nation as a whole? These are big questions that need to be answered by all of us. As a psychologist I am primarily trained to gauge the effect that a particular action has on individuals. I must warn the reader that I am on somewhat shaky ground when I deal with questions such as those that have been posed here. It is easy for a psychologist to say that manipulation by guilt is destructive to the individual. Some will argue that our national economy is geared to quick sales of mass produced products. These people would lay claim to the idea that good salesmanship involves creating a need. In that case you must coerce people to buy something they don't want.

I disagree: to me salesmanship means recognition of what human needs are. Instead of pushing products I believe we must perform more studies to find out what people really want. The goal of selling should be to satisify a human need and thereby help people become happier, more satisified, and, with some products, to even grow and develop.

It seems unlikely that the advertisers will change voluntarily. They will use whatever works. This raises the question: how well does the "guilt approach" work? Obviously it has worked. Just look at how many uneccessary products are on the market today! But who can ever predict when the public is going to rebel. Guilt makes people angry, and every so often they fight back. Business people can still remember the profit losses that followed in the clothing industry when maxi-dresses were rejected.

Let's also be aware of the growing cynicism and this often causes people to simply stop buying for long periods. Disgruntled people fight back in other ways. I was once called upon to evaluate a couple in their thirties who were caught shoplifting. They had money but said they were angry at the store because they "had been cheated." This was their way of retaliating. Is it possible that many other people feel the same way and turn to shoplifting in anger? Maybe that is one reason for the sharp increase in this crime.

Returning to my original tenet, however, people need to be free to make up their minds. While it's hard to change the marketplace, change *is* possible for individuals. Instead we will be able to have products that we really want, and feeling happier after a purchase, we may buy even more products. Joy usually begets more of the activity that produces it.

6
Guilt and our Health Habits

On the surface it might appear that guilt feelings should prompt us to care for our bodies. One could advance the argument that guilt prevents us from doing many things that are dangerous or destructive. Many people have informed me that they would never have a yearly physical examination were it not for their feelings of guilt. However, when I then ask when they had their last such exam they often say something like, "Well, I know I should go but I haven't for five years."

The idea that guilt causes us to perform constructively is against my basic thesis. I think as we examine some important areas of health the reader will come to see why I think as I do. Let's look at what happens in these various areas.

Smoking

We are all aware of the evidence that has been presented for several years that smoking is dangerous to our health. Some may argue that the evidence is not conclusive and perhaps they may have an arguable point. Most people have been convinced and there has been quite a push to get people to stop smoking. I must say at the onset that I wish the approach had been somewhat different. I feel that we need to know what human needs are satisfied (or partially appeased) by smoking and to then try to find some other habit that is not dangerous. Humans are flexible and they can generally find substitutes when necessary.

The question is about the effects of guilt. Fear may cause someone to stop something but guilt generally will not. What I have seen happen is simply this: the guilt-ridden complain more about smoking and smoke more than others. They feel guilty because they are certain they are harming themselves. They feel jumpy, tense, anxious, and angry at themselves. Some lose self-confidence: others become rebellious. In the end they desperately need that cigarette to calm down.

Then what often happens is a transfer of guilt. If the smoker can talk someone else into smoking he somehow appeases his own sagging self-concept. Others are as weak as he is: they feel that he must not be so bad. Or they exclaim "My God, I am so tense—who could blame me for smoking." Now he has found a rationalization for his objectionable activity.

What are you going to do if you wish to stop smoking? First, get rid of your guilt and look at yourself. Realize that any habit is difficult to break. Don't allow others to influence the decision you have made. If someone tries to tempt you with a cigarette, ask for a pack because you can't be expected "to stop with one." Do not be hard on yourself. Try to find some other activity to replace smoking. Some have used gum chewing: there are probably other substitutes. You may want to try a non-smoking treatment program. Most have reasonably good success for those who put effort in them. Try to find a positive course of action that will get your mind off smoking.

Drinking

I refer here to the excessive drinker and not the person who enjoys a cocktail or two with dinner or a social interaction. I think everyone has experienced the role that guilt plays in excessive drinking. First of all, many people feel inadequate in social situations. Beginning a conversation is especially disturbing.

A sense of awkwardness and inadequacy leads to feelings of guilt. "I must do something for the other person to make it up to him," the person thinks. Unfortunately his negative thoughts may well be unconscious ones and he convinces himself that he is just trying to be "sociable."

In turn, the victim becomes manipulated by his guilt. Someone is trying to be nice to him— they want to *give* him something. He may not have really wanted that drink but he dare not refuse it. His guilt won't allow him to do so. In fact, after the first drink he now owes the other fellow one. So he buys him a "repayment drink," and on and on all evening long. Neither party can linger over his drink because that might convey the impression that he isn't enjoying it.

As the drinks begin to take effect, both parties manipulate one another even further by their guilt. I have seen two drunks staggering around a bar bragging about who is more soused. They may even laugh at each other's antics, thus easing the guilt over becoming fools. When it comes time to drive home, they feel guilty because of their condition but they can't admit the fact. To do so would be to socially broadcast inadequacy and dependency. They know then they would feel even more inadequate. Most problem drinkers can't even admit that they need help, but, nevertheless are very dependent people. Somehow, they never learned how to *appropriately* depend upon people. As a consequence, they have learned how to manipulate through alcohol: generally they form relationships with people who are easily manipulated. In marriage, they find a spouse who "feels sorry for them" and cares for them when they are drunk.

One woman at a party I attended said, "My poor baby, look at him. Now I'll have to help him to the car."

"Maybe you'd better put him on a baby bottle next time," I replied.

She became angry at my remark. Apparently she needed someone who was childishly dependent upon her. (I discuss this kind of interaction in detail in another chapter.) One can see, though, how back-and-forth manipulation leads to a continual drinking problem.

Heavy drinkers are generally burdened with guilt feelings, as my professional practice attests. They want to be one type of person and recognize that they are not. A case situation might well illustrate this. John Q. was basically a man who suffered from feelings of inadequacy. He never met any of his goals. As a youth he had wanted to be an athlete and he presented evidence to show that he had physical ability. However, he lacked mental discipline and could not adhere to any solid training programs.

As a result his performance was inconsistent. For a time he played end on his high school's football team. One time he would make a spectacular catch only to drop a simple, perfectly thrown pass the next time. Gradually his coach and teammates lost confidence in him. Instead of working harder, John trained less and lost confidence in himself. He took on an "I don't care" attitude, and refused advice from everyone. During his last two years, he spent most of the time on the bench.

The pattern was repeated in John's other athletic activities. He recounted how he once lost a track meet; he was so out of shape that he blew a big lead in the final relay race.

By the time he entered college, he no longer entered sports events at all. He felt incapacitated by guilt because he was not living up to his goals. While he loved sports and had the ability to perform, he couldn't accept discipline.

In an effort to compensate, John set the career goal of becoming a wealthy businessman. He would show the world that he could be a strong, powerful successful man! Unfortunately, it didn't work out that way. John had some sales ability working for him when he joined a life insurance company. The trouble was that he was a pusher: he wanted to prove himself quickly. So a client wanted a small policy, John tried to manipulate him into a bigger one. The manipulation worked for a while but in the end the client usually cancelled the policy. Eventually John lost even the small policy-holder.

Quite naturally his superiors became increasingly disatisfied with John's work. One day, they called him in for a conference, hoping to alter John's approach. They were not successful. John resisted their criticisms. In order to be a "big man" John needed big sales. He lasted only a month longer.

For the next few years John drifted from one job to

the next. He began to pile up an impressive list of failures. Money was not coming in on a regular basis and finally John was forced to take a low-level permanent job with a large company. His salary and responsibilities were limited. John knew he had the talent and potential to do better work but he couldn't seem to get it all together. That realization made him feel guilty. Secondly, he never achieved the powerful and agressive self-image that he wanted. He was not the man that he wished to be and he felt guilty as a result.

Gradually, John turned more and more to drink. He liked the way he felt after four or five drinks. He could recapture his teenage fantasies about being a great athlete and wealthy. John said once, "The only time I feel that I am a big man is when I am drunk." In addition he liked to boast about being able to "outdrink any other man around."

Fortunately, John had a wife who would not stand for this kind of life. At one point she separated from him and refused to go back until he sought professional help. Treatment was not quick but it was very successful and John is now doing well.

The key to John's treatment was changing his self-image. As he began to feel more adequate, he didn't have to constantly prove himself. He was less dependent upon the approval of others, and he stopped his manipulation. He became more likeable, which changed his self-concept.

I would hope that most of us could avoid some of John's pitfalls, but there are many social pressures to avoid. What do we do when someone presses us to drink? Should we feel guilty saying no to something that will probably make us feel lousy? I don't think so. In addition, we shouldn't feel guilty about saying yes to something we *do* like. For example, I personally love tonic and lime. There are those who make intrusive remarks when I request that drink, especially late in an evening after I have had all the liquor I want. I simply reply, "Would you rather I drink something I don't like?" That generally stops the comments. I have heard others say, "I guess I could go next door for my tonic." As you can see, people may be manipulated by guilt just as easily when they say yes as when they say no. Don't let that happen to you. Identify the manipulative play and learn to be your own person.

Obesity and Overeating

Guilt plays a very big role in the problem of overeating. For confirmation of this, just think back to your childhood and recall what happened when you didn't eat all of your food. Many people have told me they were made to feel guilty by their parents whenever they left food on their plates. If the plate was "cleaned off," mother said, "Oh good, dear, you must have really liked that. Mother loves to see that." Well, that message was clear, wasn't it? If you want to make mother happy, eat everything on your plate. Lord knows you don't want her to feel inadequate as a housewife! One woman told me she used to eat until her stomach actually ached. Her mother then thought her daughter liked the food so much that she gave her still more.

Classically, children are made to feel guilty by being told of how the poor children of Africa (or wherever it's applicable) are starving. "These children could live on the food you waste," countless generations of children have been instructed. I must confess that I never saw the logic of that approach. Why wouldn't we conclude that it would then be more generous to eat less and ship more food to the starving people? Many children would relish that idea.

I'd like to cite another approach that engenders guilt. All children love sweets but nearly all are told that they cannot have dessert until "your plate is clean." They are made to feel guilty because they are "too full" to finish their meat and potatoes but they still have room for sweets.

In reality we all have food preferences that allow us to have our fill of one food and still desire something else. Don't adults still drink several cups of coffee after they can't finish their main course?

I know that many will object and will argue that we can't allow our children to fill up on dessert. I agree:

we need to see that children eat a balanced diet—but not every single meal and not at the expense of a jammed stomach. Dietary questions aside, my main point is that the guilt-experiencing child may well over-eat as an adult. Then his guilt continues to manipulate him into obesity. My suggestion is that we acknowledge our guilt problems so that we can simply stop eating at will.

There is another problem with obesity that also in-volves guilt. Heavy people often feel self-conscious about their appearance. I have known some who felt that their obesity made them objects of ridicule. They may have been correct because our society is very pu-nitive to the heavy person. This is especially true for women, who are expected to look young and slim.

When a person tries to lose weight, he frequently finds little encouragement. He loses a few pounds and what happens? Sue S. told me about a situation while in therapy years ago. She was informed by her doctor that she was 40 pounds overweight. Her problem had begun when she first married. Sid, her husband, liked to eat; it seemed that no matter what he ate, he still re-mained thin. However, he didn't like to eat alone and so, out of guilt, Sue joined him.

Gradually she began to gain weight; by the time she was 20 pounds overweight, Sid began to tease her about her appearance. "Where is that trim little girl I married?" he would ask. Since he always couched neg-ative statements like this in humor, it was difficult to re-spond to him. Sue felt guilty on those rare occasions when she did.

As Sue's guilt about her appearance was accompan-ied by depression, feelings of despair caused her to eat even more, and she gained still more weight. Sue be-came so guilt-ridden that she began to feel uncomforta-ble with social contact. Her withdrawal precipitated more eating binges.

Sue tried many times to lose weight but one doesn't lose 40 pounds overnight. Everytime she lost three pounds, she looked to Sid for support. She wanted en-couragement but instead he made negative comments. "Are you sure you lost those three pounds?" he would ask. Feeling even more guilt-ridden, Sue would go off her diet. However, defining Sue's problem made the solution quite simple. She needed to reduce her guilt and she needed support from Sid. Once both conditions were met she stuck to her diet and became a much happier person.

It is important to realize how overweight people are routinely manipulated. If someone feels guilty about an obesity problem, he can lessen his guilt by pointing out someone else whom he feels is worse off. He attacks those who remind him of his failings. He may seek out others who are more overweight than he is because that makes him look better. Those who are themselves easily manipulated by guilt then become targets.

In addition, the person who goes on a diet has accomplished something that many other people are unable to do. That arouses the guilt of jealous people. They feel better if they can sabotage the diet program. If they can demoralize the dieter, then perhaps his resultant guilt will drive him to eat more.

We notice a similar situation with individuals who regularly control their diet. People will try to make them feel guilty because of their restraint. One woman has told me that several resentful co-workers have openly expressed jealousy of her trim appearance. One added, "Most of all, I dislike dining with you, Jane. You always watch what you eat. That upsets me."

Fortunately, Jane is a rather guilt-free person. She answered simply, "Don't watch." However, many who are less secure fail. Consciously we can all make a decision: we won't let this happen to us. Are we going to be so spineless that we allow others to tell us what to eat? I don't think any of us want to give up that much freedom.

I would strongly suggest that you be firm. Gently tell the bully not to worry so much about what you do. I like to ask directly if the person is trying to make me feel guilty and point out that it isn't working. He will most certainly have to deny his true motive but will probably stop his manipulation. If he says yes, render him impotent by saying: "Since I now know your intention, I'll make allowances for it." There is no need to say any of this with great anger. Your goal is not to crush the person but only to stop his objectionable behavior.

Accident Prone

There are some people who can't do anything without harming themselves. Often, they appear to be careful, thoughtful individuals who plan things out (and still everything goes wrong.) The unfortunate term "born loser" seems to describe this group.

I had the misfortune to know someone like this many years ago. I often wonder how I survived the friendship. Bill H. was the overly "helpful" kind of person who always managed to bring out the worst in me. There were times when I used to scream, "Please Bill, just leave it where it is, I will get it!" But he wouldn't: he just had to help. On one occasion, he insisted on helping me unlock my car. I was bringing some supplies into a summer cottage and he decided to take 3-gallon cans of paint out of my car. He carried them to the door and then yelled back to me that the cottage was locked.

"Naturally it is, Bill," I said, "I have been gone for three hours." I tossed him the keys and saw him unlock the door. I erroneously assumed that he had taken the paint inside the cottage and did not see the cans on the doorstep as I walked up the steps loaded with other supplies. When my feet collided with the cans I nearly went headfirst through the door.

Then there was the time that I moved all my belongings from my school dormitory to the summer cottage. I had rented a lug that attached to my car so that I could take everything in one load. Bill arrived at my cottage just in time to offer "help." Somehow I let him talk me into driving the car and lug up to the back door. By so doing, he reasoned, we wouldn't have to carry things for so great a distance.

In theory it sounded great: in practice it was disaster. We had to drive over wet ground and shortly became stuck in the soft ground. While I got out to inspect the situation Bill slipped into the driver's seat to make one last desperate attempt to extricate the car. As I was bending down to look at the tires he started the motor. Suddenly I was covered with mud. Bill's reaction was predictable: "Sorry, Harry, I was just trying to help."

We struggled with the car for a long, long time until it finally became obvious that we couldn't get it free. So I returned to the cottage to call a tow truck. I didn't realize that Bill was out there still trying to help. He let some of the air out of the rear tires because he had read that by so doing one increases the friction on the tires. Typically, though, that didn't work either. When the tow truck arrived they did quickly get the car out, but when the driver saw the flat tires he informed me that I couldn't drive on them. I was obliged to hire him to change both tires so I could again use the car.

While we waited for the tow truck, Bill kept talking about how everything went wrong in his life. He indicated how hard he tried to work to help others; how he really didn't mind that his shoes were muddy because he was so concerned with my welfare. He even stated that he could well imagine that I was pretty angry at him.

This approach instills guilt in the victim while not allowing him to vent his anger. Feeling anguish and sorrow for his friend's failings, the victim is unable to feel sorry for *himself*. It's easier to lie to the manipulator than to state one's true feelings. Reassured that things aren't that bad after all, the manipulator secures the ego enhancement he was after all along.

My last encounter with Bill illustrates his motives. One day when I was replacing ceiling tile in a basement apartment I had just rented, Bill came over. We were having some pleasant conversation, but Bill simply couldn't let it go at that. He started moving one of the step ladders and soon was climbing the ladder to help remove the old tile.

Glancing over, I happened to note that each time Bill finished a section he placed his hammer on the ladder top. Then leaving it there he climbed down and moved the ladder. That is a highly dangerous thing to do: as you carry the ladder, any sideways tilt will bring the hammer down upon you. I explained the danger to Bill just as he was moving the ladder.

"I'll be okay, I can—aaah," he screamed as the hammer struck him in the head. The claw part of the hammer raked his forehead, giving him a nasty cut.

I rushed to his aid, and for the next 40 minutes we held cold towels over the cut. The whole time Bill wore a smile on his face. He had shed blood in my service and now he was getting attention. He kept reminding me over and over, "It will be o.k., it's just a little cut," and that he was so sorry that he couldn't help me anymore. His help consisted of having removed six ceiling tiles, something I could have done in roughly eight minutes. As a result of the injury I lost over an hour.

Bill was just beginning his hard luck story when he said, "I guess I was lucky I might have been——." He never finished the word "killed" because he saw the gleam in my eye.

"You wouldn't hit an injured man would you, Harry?" Bill said, pleading for sympathy.

"Let me think for a moment, Bill," I returned.

I knew then that I had to have a heart-to-heart talk with Bill. There was simply no point in continuing our present relationship. Thinking it over, I decided that I had never liked listening to him talk about all of the things he did for me. If he wanted to help, that was one thing, but I didn't want to hear about it later.

It was obvious that what he achieved was "secondary" gain from his many injuries and mishaps. I realized I no longer wanted to be in his debt. Especially since any time he "helped" me, the job ran at least an hour longer than it would be otherwise. I couldn't take it any longer and wondered why it had taken so long to make that decision.

I sat down with Bill and talked about the way things were going to have to change. I told him that I liked to get things done quickly and that somehow when we worked together it never worked out that way. Sure, his intentions were probably good (on a conscious level) but I had to judge by the final outcome. It was undeniable fact that we did not work well together.

Bill reacted defensively for a time. He insisted I was a friend and as such he wanted to help. It would be hard for him to sit back and just watch me work. He would change; he knew he could; I just didn't have faith in him, and so on. I let him talk but finished by saying, "Sorry Bill, but this is the way it has to be."

Gradually he was able to accept my decision and his defenses rose once again. "I was a loner," he said. "I liked to do things by myself, I liked working extra hard. . . ." I simply responded that perhaps he was right but whatever the reason it had to be that way. The most stringent test of our friendship came on those occasions when another friend worked with me. Bill had a kind of sibling rivalry and would try to manipulate by saying it was unfair to let someone else help if he couldn't. I never gave long defensive explanations: I stuck to my guns and Bill and I again got along well.

I had considered talking to Bill about his continual use of guilt and his self-defeatism. I decided against it. His defenses were so well fortified that he never took a long, hard look at himself. Then at a time when I felt he might be open to some professional advice he moved away.

Closely related is the individual who "drives dangerously" by refusing to do anything about an incipient heart condition. Characteristically, they remain overweight, eat unwisely and get either too much or too little exercise. Sometimes they drink excessively to relish driving dangerously in their condition. Frequently, they brag about the risks they take.

How does manipulation by guilt enter into the lives of these people? What exactly are they hoping to gain through their reckless actions? We can find out by looking at individual cases with attention to ends and means.

Wilson H. is a 45-year-old man who is overweight and has a heart condition. After noting an incidence of chest pain and minor changes in his electro-cardiography Wilson's doctor warned him to cut down his smoking. But Wilson hasn't heeded any of this advice.

In fact, Wilson enjoys bragging at social gatherings about all the advice he has received. After announcing that he isn't following any of this advice, he frequently jokes that there are more old drunks than old doctors!

Wilson is really scared of his condition but can't admit it. Feelings of fear bring on feelings of guilt. By showing the world that he isn't afraid of anything, he doesn't have to deal with his guilt problem and if others buy Wilson's act, maybe he can, too.

Secondly, Wilson needs attention. The more that people respond to his act, the more he can drain off guilt and anxiety. Wilson feels important when someone tells him to "be careful." He is a master at provoking guilt reactions and thereby developing protagonists. If someone can be defeated in argument, then he has seemingly strengthened his decision to avoid appropriate health measures. The concern of others causes him to feel important.

Initially, I became aware of Wilson through mutual friends; later, however, he applied for long-term psychotherapy. That is a form of treatment that aims at comprehensive personality change and is expected to last quite sometime. Wilson began the request by telling me he was "here at the suggestion of his boss." I have my doubts that you can help me, Doctor," he stated in a challenging manner.

"So do I, Wilson, for several reasons. First of all I doubt that you really want to change your personality. Secondly, it would be my impression that you may not be around sufficiently long to profit from a long-term therapy." Wilson began to argue: how could I turn him down? He needed help: what kind of professional was I? If I could only give him a chance he would show me. As you may detect, he was really trying to do a job on me. If I could be manipulated by guilt feelings, I would be had just like everyone else he encountered. Significantly, though. I would have failed him.

I explained to Wilson that a therapist must make certain decisions to effect proper treatment. (Otherwise, why waste the time and money?) I carefully outlined how he was trying to manipulate me. As long as he did that, he could not profit from therapy; of course, I would not yield. I told him I felt he wanted to be in therapy merely to satisify the demands of his boss. Therapy can only succeed when a person has a sincere desire to change. From all indications, this was not the case with Wilson. He seemed to grasp intellectually what I told him—which pleased me. To my surprise he returned a month later. He was somewhat more motivated because there were new signs of heart problems. He was even able to acknowledge his fears. I saw this as a good beginning.

I explained to Wilson that I felt he needed a therapist with a medical background. I had a hunch he might need tranquilizers occasionally to calm himself without alcohol. In addition it seemed advantageous to work with a physician who could speak knowledgeably about the symptoms of Wilson's heart. I indicated to Wilson that I was referring him to a psychiatrist acquaintance.

Wilson briefly tried to manipulate me for the last time. He knew I was a good therapist and he liked me. He didn't want to go to a stranger.

"You will like Dr. N.," I told him. "He is a very capable man; he does good work; and he is very personable." I made the statement with so much finality that Wilson gave in to my professional judgement. He began his treatment program and I am happy to say things went very well. I think there are some important lessons to be learned from the approach that Dr. N. used with Wilson.

It was not possible for Wilson to manipulate Dr. N. When the patient finds he can no longer meet success with his old approach he begins to look for a new one. Wilson could not get more attention from his therapist by self destructive behavior.

Secondly, Dr. N. told him he would drop him as a patient if he saw Wilson working against what therapy sought to achieve. If gains were to be made they had to take place over two equally important fronts: namely medical and psychological. Drinking, for example, worked counter to therapy and could not, therefore, coexist with therapy. A type of contact was established and Wilson knew as a result what was to be expected of him. He received support from his therapist when he did well. He received no sympathy when he acted self-destructively. In less than a year Wilson's whole behavior patterns had changed.

I recall a similar personality type who made a sudden

change without therapy. Hal was normally a quiet, passive man and he hated himself for it. He made a habit
of informing everyone that he "hated passive men."
Most individuals knew who Hal was referring to. They
felt sorry for him and kept silent as he became a habitual drunk. He became boisterous, a braggert, and tried
to pick fights. The only reason he didn't get his face
punched in was that everyone felt guilty standing up to
him. He was too weak to hurt.

Hal's biggest play for attention came when it was
time to drive home. He would never allow his wife to
drive because it would make him feel "little." He was
such a crazy driver when drunk that no one would ever
leave a party at the same time Hal did. With overabundant bravado he would enter his car and then roar out
of the driveway.

The turning point finally came when Hal nearly hit a
neighbor's child one evening after a party. For the good
of everyone this neighbor did not feel guilty as he
called the police. Fortunately there was a squad car
nearby which intercepted Hal. He was so drunk that he
could barely stand up. As a result he was arrested and
charged with drunken driving. Some of the people who
had been at the party laughed at the incident. Tragically, that offers encouragement to persons like Hal. The
couple who had arranged the party stopped laughing
when they found they could be charged with a crime
for serving liquor to a drunk. When that fact became
common knowledge none of Hal's friends supported his
reckless behavior.

Should they have been manipulated by guilt feelings?
Most certainly not. What if Hal had killed that child, or
someone else? Or even himself? We are all aware of
the fatality statistics ocasioned by drunken driving. Yet
many of us fail to take appropriate action because we
feel guilty being a stool pigeon. I have often wondered
if we'd react the same way to crime prevention, but that
is another story.

The Malpractice Potential

Recently I heard of another form of manipulation by guilt that may have dangerous implications for the future. As a psychologist I am naturally concerned about the malpractice situation in this country, but this affects all of us. As suits proliferate, the cost of medical and psychological treatment rise out of necessity. Currently many doctors are paying as much as $40,000 per year for malpractice insurance. To cover the climbing rates doctors will be forced to charge higher fees.

Believe it or not, manipulation by guilt can actually raise the cost of medical care. Recently a doctor friend of mine told me he was threatened with a law suit. He had been talking with a neighbor friend who complained about pain in his shoulder. The neighbor asked what might cause such pain and was told that a number of things might. He offered to drive over to his office and examine his friend. No, the friend was in a hurry, and said, "Gee Doc, if you could only suggest something — it hurts, real bad."

The doctor reported that he had felt a little guilty hearing about how the guy was suffering.

"Well, all right, you might try putting some moist heat on it," the doctor suggested, "but let me know if the pain doesn't go away."

It didn't go away; in fact, it became much worse. The pain spread all over the man's chest and when breathing became difficult, his wife took him to the emergency unit of the local hospital. They diagnosed that the man was suffering from a previously unknown heart condition.

After a speedy recovery, the man began to think in terms of a law suit. His lawyer agreed that he had a case. Treatment had been suggested without a thorough diagnosis. The treatment turned out to be faulty. The man initiating the suit didn't stop to consider that he pressed for a suggestion, that he probably had other symptoms that he didn't mention, and that the doctor offered to see him at his office (even though it was not during his regular working time).

I think this kind of manipulation is dangerous to both

doctor and patient. I am beginning to feel doctors may be unable to give casual advice anymore.

Psychosomatic Disorders

Many people mistakenly believe that a psychosomatic illness is an imaginary malady manufactured by the patient to gain attention. It is more properly understood as a physical complaint caused or aggravated by emotional states: for example, the peptic ulcer.

My wife once had a friend, Jan, who had an ulcer that was felt by her doctor to be psychosomatic. She was a very anxious guilt-ridden woman who resisted her friends' suggestions that she needed treatment. She made them feel guilty by claiming they were as bad as her doctor. "You all feel I'm crazy," Jan would declare. Then everyone would reassure her and subsequently support her decision not to go to a therapist. Later they all felt guilty knowing they had failed her.

Once I met Jan at a party that my wife and I attended. At her request I explained that a psychosomatic disorder may result from a valiant attempt to contain our psychological tension. Jan was relieved that I didn't think she was crazy. I did tell her as gently as I could that I felt she was very foolish not to seek professional help. In turn, Jan tried to make me feel guilty but it didn't work. I stuck to my guns, feeling she could take the truth. I am delighted to say that Jan has obtained the care she needed and seems to be doing well.

Another man I know has a similar type of disorder—a terrible fear of flying. Every time someone plans a trip he includes himself, only to cancel out as soon as the plane is ready to leave the ground. He then manipulates everyone around him to feel guilty because he "can't stand to fly." Mutual friends have told me that entire vacations have been cancelled because the other men felt so much guilt.

Why should they let themselves be manipulated by someone who refuses to try to change. This man lives in New York and as a result I seldom see him. On the few occasions when I have, I have suggested a program run by a friend of mine, Dr. Burton Siegel. Dr. Siegel is a psychologist, flies a private plane, and from what I can ascertain, does an excellent job with his program, Overcoming the Fear of Flying. Would it not be worth the low price to attempt to rid oneself of this disorder? I guess not—not as long as friends can be manipulated by guilt. Maybe when the friends can cease to be manipulated the man will seek professional help.

Manipulation Through Illness

Of course, no chapter such as this would be complete until there was some discussion regarding manipulation through illness. Probably every one of us has known dozens of people who use this ploy. Much of human interaction is based upon it; clearly, it is dangerous to both the manipulator and the victim. Neither can live full, active lives.

The first example that comes to mind is a young graduate student, Paul D. He was small, frail and had a sickly appearance. Generally regarded as passive, he had a very sharp tongue. Paul hated sports and athletes: he regarded himself as "intellectual" and did seem very bright. But he was quick to let people know what his opinions were—and that he disliked most activities that "the common folk" liked.

I can still remember my excitement when one of my favorite teams, the Brooklyn Dodgers, finally beat the formidable Yankees in the World Series. Paul thought I was being ridiculous at the time. I felt he didn't understand the frustration of being a Dodger fan at World Series time. Dodger fans have a way of popping up all over the place, and even though Purdue University is in the Midwest there were many there. We managed to get together for a celebration party and somehow Paul was invited. Maybe we Dodger fans are masochists.

When Paul arrived we were all celebrating the marvelous victory of our team: their first ever in the big series.

True to his character, Paul loudly proclaimed it was "stupid" to care that much what a group of paid athletes did. I allowed that Dodger fans had never been known as brilliant. Maybe that was why we stuck with a team that had a habit of building up our hopes just to let us down again.

Paul did not make himself popular at the party, but I was soon to come to know that he never did anywhere. He was a real joy killer and his sharp tongue often got him in real trouble. He provoked people to the point where they were ready to physically attack him. I saw it happen the night of our big victory celebration. He was not a part of baseball and he would try to make anyone who was different feel guilty.

Naturally, many people took offense, and I heard one young man say that if he didn't get an apology he was going to smash Paul's face. Paul immediately had an asthma attack. He wheezed, coughed, and sputtered. His antagonism began to crumble.

"See what you have done," Paul accused. "I could die from one of these attacks."

Suddenly Paul was the center of attention and nearly everyone was rushing to his aid. He kept a subtle attack going on the man who had threatened him. In a short time Paul was the hero and the other man who had continuously been called "stupid" was the bully.

Paul clearly came off the victor in the first encounter that I witnessed. He never apologized for his abusive behavior and the other man did. In addition, Paul made his victim look bad because he never accepted his apology. That was a constant maneuver of Paul's. He could provoke people with his sharp tongue but they were never allowed to fight back. To do so would be to cause an asthma attack.

Paul used his asthma in a variety of other ways, too. When he was left out of a conversation he became at first fidgety. He would interrupt but if that were unsuccessful he would draw attention to himself with coughing and wheezing. Pretty soon all eyes would turn to him with sympathy. Then the wheezing would begin to subside and he would center all verbal attention on "his condition."

It was truly amazing how long Paul got away with his manipulation. I saw a number of supervisors back off when he began to have yet another attack. Paul did not make friends and certainly no one respected him but he went right on manipulating.

One day, however, this all came to an end. Paul had made a serious mistake with a patient and this had to be called to his attention. A female supervisor began a discussion with him and Paul went into one of his fabled attacks. Instead of backing off, though, his supervisor mentioned that perhaps Paul couldn't take criticism from a woman. That he could never publicly admit. The wheezing began to subside.

Each time Paul began to show signs of an attack the supervisor said, "Paul, if you aren't up to this we can take a break and come back to it." She did not plan to drop the discussion, she wouldn't be manipulated, and it was left up to Paul to get himself under control.

I think that is the key to handling this kind of manipulation. You point out what is taking place and you do not alter your approach. You are telling the person that you will not be sidetracked and their technique will no longer work. Generally they will soon get the message and cease in their attempt to manipulate. An approach such as Paul used works only as long as other people play by his rules.

Psychological Manipulation

The age of psychology has produced a new variety of manipulation and it is terribly destructive. It plays a part in marital, sexual, child-parent, and school manipulation. Instead of declaring that we dislike some form of behavior we label it. Thus, riding a motorcycle is no longer called dangerous. Instead we say that only the immature rebel this way.

When a woman chooses a career, we no longer say we hate to see her leave her home. Instead we point out that a high percent of working women are neurotic or driven by "penis envy." Now, who would want to be guilty of that!

Perhaps it is because I am a psychologist that I hate this kind of manipulation more than other varieties. People are often defenseless, partly because they feel that the statements are founded in scientific research. And, perhaps they may be. Rarely, however, are the results of the study carefully applied to the particular person upon whom they are focused.

Let's take one case in point to illustrate. A colleague of mine has stated that female psychologists and psychiatrists are in the practice *because* they are neurotic. He worded his statement in such a manner so as to imply that all such women are motivated solely by neurosis.

I asked one day why he made that statement in such strong language. He quoted a study showing a higher suicide rate for women in this field as compared to housewives. Now when we look at the study what does it actually show in regard to the individual? Not very much. You can't diagnose an individual from group membership *unless* every member of that group fits the diagnosis. And they almost never really do.

I tried to tell this man that one of the nicest, healthiest, supportive, *people* I have ever known is a lady psychiatrist. That made no difference to him. In plain fact he does not really like women.

I believe that many people today are manipulated out of something they like or at least emotionally turned off. They can't have fun because of the psychological name-calling. It is particularly destructive because of the indirect quality of the attack.

When that happens I suggest a direct attack. It is "hostile" to point out someone's "neurosis" unless you are asked. What kind of psychologist would I be if I deliberately told people they were "acting out, neurotic, immature," or doing something because of "irrational motivation." Would that really help people? So when someone does this he or she is showing their guilt, jealousy, envy, or anger. I would suggest that you directly question their motivation for their statements. I can tell you that my colleague stopped his unsolicited comments when I asked if he disliked being around women.

Do your own thing, and as long as it brings more pleasure than pain, fine. Don't overanalyze yourself and never allow others to do it to you *unless* you have asked them to. And oh, be careful who you ask!

7

Guilt, Manipulation
and Athletic Competition

Generally, most people would assume athletics is one area that is free from guilt. Sports are fun, we tell ourselves, and there is nothing to feel guilty about when we are out running or throwing a ball around. Unfortunately, this is not always the case. In order to explore this, let us examine the basic reasons why people engage in sports.

The Need for Physical Activity

National interest in physical fitness is cyclical. In wartime, interest characteristically rises: everyone seems interested in trying to increase endurance and lung capacity. We adopt slogans such as "a strong America means strong people." Then when the war ends, so does our desire for a Spartan culture. We overeat, become overweight and sedentary, while we stress intellectual pursuits.

Then suddenly physical fitness mania sweeps the nation. We become a nation of joggers, tennis players and golf buffs. This lasts for a while but never for long, to be sure.

Why such extremes of interest? I think there are some very logical reasons for this and, of course, guilt plays a big part. For one thing, characteristically wide swings in behavior are a reflection of manipulation by guilt. For instance, when a noted authority tells us we must exercise, we usually follow like sheep. After a while, though, we rebel against his authority and go back to our old ways.

My own personal experiences corroborate this. I remember being told in several high school gym classes that "healthy minds require healthy bodies." Now, could anyone possibly question that? Besides, we thought we were going to have fun. Probably 99 percent of us had already experienced the fun of sports on our neighborhood sandlots.

Our expectations were very short-lived, however. On our first day with the instructor, a former army sergeant, we were told that we wouldn't find *his* program fun. We were "soft, lazy, undisciplined, and ignorant." His message was: We didn't know how to get ourselves in shape.

The young men in the group reacted two ways. Some accepted the statement without question: exercise was good but it was not fun. They would follow the program to his authoritative pose for their own good. This group would cooperate with the instructor but they wouldn't enjoy it.

The second group reacted very rebelliously. Clearly, only force could compel their cooperation. They would try to sabotage the program in every possible way. For example, if the teacher looked away for a moment, they'd quit exercising. In this way, they would get even with the instructor but at a great personal cost.

Initially the instructor established levels of fitness to grade our skills. A norm of 25 pushups was established for each boy. There were special credits for anyone who could do more. The boys who were poorly coordinated found the goal of 25 push-ups excessive: they may have completed their requirement but their form was terrible. Many of these boys were ridiculed by the teacher—as well as the class. Feeling guilty, these victims were manipulated into trying harder but their self images dropped to a new low.

What are the results of this strategy? Predictably, the boys who were ridiculed probably learned to hate any form of athletics. Those who rebelled probably continue to do so today. The group that cooperated learned that sports are "necessary" but not fun. As a result they are periodically manipulated into athletic programs; after a brief time, they tire and leave.

What went wrong here? When all available evidence suggests that a regular physical activity program is good for nearly everyone, why do some people still shun it? And why do we assume that athletics aren't going to be fun? I am quite certain that if we used a different approach and showed people how to have fun, we would have more permanent participants. The second improvement would be to allow a wider selection of sporting activity. Not every person likes a contact sport or a competitive sport. Allowing youngsters to select a sport that fits their personality and body type encourages them to enjoy themselves. Finally, teachers should not enforce norms as inflexible standards. In this way, the child is not penalized for being different or uncoordinated.

Once these changes are made, people will exercise of their own volition. Note that I said *people*: I feel girls can and should be allowed to enjoy sporting activity. They should not be manipulated into a mold and always made to believe they are intruding into a "man's world."

Status and Social Imitation

Unfortunately many people are made to feel guilty because they don't fit into a mold. A father who has been athletic may feel that his son must be the same. The only time the two communicate is when the son fulfills the father's fantasies. Since the guilt-ridden son can never enjoy himself, he will likely follow one of two directions. He will be manipulated into conforming and subsequently leave the sport at the first opportunity. Or he will rebel and hate sports.

What can be done to avoid this unhappy situation? Let me quote the words of one of the finest coaches I have ever known. He is Earl Stewart Jr., golf coach at Southern Methodist University in Dallas. I have always loved golf and wondered what the best way was to introduce our two boys to the game. Earl suggested that I do little in the way of formal instruction when they are young. "Let them see that you enjoy the game," Earl suggested. "Let them find their own joy and, in so doing, if nature intended, they will probably play the game well." The best I can do is to pass on this very sage advice.

Competition

Not all sports are inherently competitive but, of course, any human activity can be *made* competitive. By its nature, football has to be competitive; on the other hand, fishing, golf and swimming go either way.

Competition is both a blessing and a curse. I think that it is healthy and growth producing for both men and women to enjoy the thrill of competition. What is psychologically not sound, however, is competition for the sakes of building a self-image. Typically the insecure individuals look to sports in order to feel worthwhile. Sports becomes an ego crutch. In this situation, winning and losing are more important than how you play the game.

On the other hand, some people enjoy competition and use it to seek steady improvement. Success enhances rather then props up the ego. (These individuals already possess a steady self-image.) Just as failure doesn't destroy them, success doesn't bring self-deception.

Given the positive aspects of competition, what's wrong with it? For an answer, let's look at young women and sports. Women are told by nearly everyone that they should not be assertive or aggressive. Society says this behavior isn't proper for young ladies. They must be prim, proper, stuffy, passive, and compliant.

The young girl knows from experience that she enjoys running, jumping, and throwing just as boys do. In most cases she wants to be able to compete with others. For proof of this, just look at the girls in your neighborhood that organize and play competitive games. And for that matter, wasn't hopscotch always competitive? And even jump rope? These are classic games for girls.

Sooner or later, though, the young girl learns to feel guilty about competition. Most withdraw from competition in early adolescence. For the few that remain, there is great pressure to succeed. If you are going to compete, so the message goes, you had better be great. Few people will make it easy for the young female athlete. Other girls will start pushing her to excell so they can share her deeds vicariously. As pressure mounts, failure can produce terrible guilt reactions. Either the girl bends under tension or is pushed to work harder than she truly wants.

The young boy is manipulated in a different fashion. Often pressured from his parents, he is probably "pushed" by his coaches as well. Only a good performance is one that wins. When he doesn't do well, he "lets his team down." As you might expect, the guilt is unbearable.

I saw several youngters in psychotherapy who were terribly upset because of occurances on the athletic field. One boy, Wilson S., who had begun stuttering, seemed deeply depressed for a 16-year-old boy. A fidgety boy, he even seemed to be developing self-destructive tendencies. While Wilson was certainly not suicidal, his alert parents told me that he appeared to be doing things to hurt himself. While he had always had a neat appearance, he had recently begun to dress in a sloppy manner. Wearing clothes that were not color-coordinated, he was teased by peers. He accepted the ridicule and even seemed to initiate it by making many self-derogatory remarks.

I talked to Wilson to find what was troubling him. Clearly a guilt-ridden boy, he commented, "I always seem to let people down."

"Would you give me an example, Wilson?" I asked.

There was a pause and then his whole expression saddened. He told me how he had personally lost an important football game last year. Losing 7-6 with several minutes to play, he first dropped a little screen pass that would have allowed his team to make a first down. His coach gambled and while faking a punt on a fourth down, the kicker ran for a first down.

Then the team began to make yardage and gain momentum. On one play Wilson caught a short pass that resulted in a crucial first down. But, in the process he hurt his ankle and went to the bench. During a time-out his coach told him that, hurt or not, he had to go back into the game. The injury was judged not serious (as later medical opinion verified).

"Our ends have been covered all day, Wilson," the coach said in front of the team. "You are the only man we have with enough speed to come out of the backfield and catch a long pass. We have only 30 seconds, but you can do it for your team."

"Yeah, Wilson, we know you can do it," echoed several teammates.

So Wilson went back into the game, but he recalled feeling tense. He felt too guilt-ridden to complain about his ankle. He tested the ankle on the next play from scrimmage and it seemed strong. Then came his real test. On the next play he faked to his right and began running full speed downfield. He suddenly found himself out in the open, and as he turned he saw the quarterback cocking his arm to throw. With beautiful precision, the quarterback fired a long, arching pass down field just as he was being tackled. The pass was perfectly thrown and landed right in Wilson's arms. Wilson had the ball but unfortunately he took his eyes off it, just for a second, to see where the pass defenders were. As he did, the ball slipped through his fingers and fell to the ground. The huge crowd was stunned. Victory had turned to ignominious defeat.

In the locker room after the game, Wilson sat tearfully by himself. No one said anything to him and he quietly dressed and left the scene. As he was walking out the coach said, "Well, son, I don't know how many times I have told you to never take your eyes off that ball. Sure, you might have been tackled, but we still had time for a field goal if you had caught the ball."

I talked to Wilson at length about the game but it took me a long time to find out that Wilson had scored his team's only touchdown for the day. Why would he forget such an important detail? How about the place kicker who had missed the extra point? If blame was being assessed, didn't he merit his share? Apparently, not in Wilson's mind, because Wilson was unfortunately very susceptible to manipulation by guilt.

I have personally seen several incidents involving my own two boys. When Billy was seven-years-old, he was asked to swim backstroke on our country club's swim team. Billy has always been an excellent free-styler—in fact, he won the league championship for his age group when he was six. In his age bracket he has always had a better than average breaststroke. One day, his coach Bob decided that Billy, a natural swimmer, could do well with the backstroke. There was one major problem, however. Billy tried the stroke and didn't enjoy it. He is a very competitive boy who tries to do well and he found, coming towards the end of the pool, he couldn't gauge where he was. Where other youngsters of his age automatically slowed their stroke, Billy did not. As a result, he whacked his head on the cement gutter several times.

I knew none of this but when I came home from the office one day, Billy had a question for me. "Dad, when you were a boy, did you like the backstroke?"

This is generally how my boys indicate that they want to discuss something.

As it happened, I did *not* like the backstroke during my competitive days. Like Billy, I have a sinus allergy and I always managed to get water into my nose. Billy informed me that he hated the backstroke; I suggested he relay that message to his coach. I did tell Bill that sometimes we need to do things we don't like. At the same time, I indicated I didn't want him to be manipulated.

A week later, his coach ran into me at a local store. He came over to tell me his side of the situation. He had other backstroke swimmers but he wanted to force Billy to swim this stroke. He felt Billy might gain several points for him in the championship. Forcing Billy to swim hardly seemed necessary to me; our team usually won by several hundred points. But Bob was the coach and I hesitated to interfere.

However, he has showed no hesitance in interfering with our family life. He told me Billy had said that, like his dad, he didn't like backstroke. I told Bob that I was only backing up Billy's true feelings.

"I know you are a psychologist," Bob persisted, "but truth isn't the best approach with kids on some occasions. Now Billy insists he will swim the other three strokes but not backstroke. Your truthful answer has made my job harder."

So now it was out in the open. Both Billy and I were supposed to feel guilty. I should have lied to him. Angrily, (and without guilt) I replied:

"I have seen from your methods that you don't value truth. That is your decision. I'm sure when you finally do have children they will reflect that. My boys, however, will continue to learn both truth and humility from me!" That ended the incident; Billy made his contribution to the team by doing what he enjoyed doing.

Frequently several members of a family have similar personality traits. Bob's brother Mick also worked at the country club as a swimming coach. My older boy, Buddy, had an unpleasant run-in with him. Now, Buddy is an excellent swimmer. He has lost only two races in all the years he has swam the breaststroke competition.

When Buddy was seven, he was matched against eight-year-olds in competition. He had some very tough competition, especially in free-style, which was not his best stroke. All during the dual meets which preceded the championship, Buddy was placed in the free-style relay. I was surprised because there were four boys who swam faster. I could see that week by week Buddy was building up his hopes of winning the championship.

I tried to prepare him for the possibility that he wouldn't compete in the relay when championship rolled around. Buddy would reply that Mick told him he would be in the event "if we clinched first place." Since the relays came last in the swimming meet, there was a good chance that our team would have "clinched" victory.

This was what actually happened. Expectantly, Buddy got ready for the main event. When Mick walked by, Buddy said, "Well, I made it, didn't I?"

Mick walked right by him not saying a word. When Buddy persisted, Mick responded that it wouldn't be fair to the other boys who were faster than Buddy.

"You don't want me to cheat them, do you, Buddy?" he asked.

"No, I guess not," Buddy replied and walked away, disheartened.

The coach had a point—the very same point I was trying to make with Buddy all year. Buddy knew that only the best should be allowed to compete but couldn't accept it emotionally. If he had been adequetely prepared for that realization, he could have handled it rather well. Youngsters face reality well, but, often it is the adult who fails in his duty. He obscures reality to the extent that the younger person can't recognize it.

The following year the country club was blessed with a new coach, Don Johnson. One of the finest people I have known, he also happens to be an excellent coach. He never manipulates by guilt, but helps each youngster see where he stands and what he can do. He once told me his goal is to help each youngster develop his own talent and fulfill his inner potential. Don doesn't only stress winning. I have seen him praise a youngster who came in last if he felt the youngster did well by his own standards.

In addition, both boys and girls swim on the team, though not against each other. (The girls are not handicapped.) Girls are not punished for wanting to be competitive. It is indeed a marvelous sight to see both sexes working together and helping each other in a sporting contest.

Eddie Pounder is another excellent coach who concentrates on making hockey enjoyable. He told me that while he tries to win games, he is mostly concerned with each boy's development as a player. With his assistant, Don Boot, the two men build confidence through constructive criticism. They may quietly take a boy aside and tell him where he erred, but never with anger. Eddie once said that these young boys learn more from their mistakes than from their great plays.

I believe we need more men in sports like Johnson, Boots, Pounders and the Stewarts. There are probably many reasons, however, why we don't attract more people like this to coaching. Salaries are low; parents

are pushy; and our society as a whole clamors for win-
ners.

I have read some interesting books lately about
"psyching" or intimidating an opponent. Personally, I
wonder why we have become so desperate to win. It always seemed to me that the point of sports was to
have fun, not to intimidate someone.

We all know people who are vulnerable to this sort of
manipulation. For instance, recently I met Bill W., who
had a problem with his aggressiveness and always
seemed guilt—ridden. He was literally afraid of doing
anything aggressive. For example, when playing golf,
he began to feel guilty when he was way ahead of his
opponent. He realized that he could be easily manipulated by his opponents, even in a friendly match. Comments such as, "Hey Bill, give a guy a chance," often
slowed-down his game.

In conversation, Bill revealed that his father always
felt sorry for the underdog. On one occasion, Bill won a
golf match rather handily and his father said, "Boy, I
bet that guy feels mighty low!" Of course, this is the
kind of remark that made Bill feel guilty about being a
winner.

As his competitive golf career progressed, Bill's
game began to slide when he had a sizable lead. Characteristically, he allowed his opponent to gain momentum. As fear set in, Bill would become addled and his
game would fall apart. "Bill blew another match," his
teammates would say. Gradually he began to develop
into a born loser.

Eventually I got Bill to realize that no one ever has to
angonize over defeat. When you begin to lose, you can
simply try harder. If defeat comes your way, there is always another day. You don't have to feel humiliated if
you did your best. By the same token, the winner does
not actually do anything to the loser. Bill didn't force
the loser to agonize over defeat or to play the game. If
defeat is that devastating, why play in the first place?

I have seen some improvement in Bill both in sports
and at work. He is better able to do his own thing and
doesn't worry excessively about the other guy. He
deals directly with his aggressive feeling. Recently I

heard him say something that summarizes his new outlook.

A number of foursomes had bunched up on a short par three hole. Bill had apparently been playing very well and his team in a "Scotch Foursome" was well ahead. Bill was on the tee setting up a shot. Before he was ready, one of his opponents said Bill was unmerciful that day and should show a little compassion.

"At least you guys may learn to be graceful losers," he retorted. "Stop your whining." With that comment, he hit his ball right next to the cup.

In athletics, as well as other endeavors, guilt is an obstacle to success. You can manage your guilt easily by coming to terms with your competitive impulses. After all, you aren't out there to kill someone; you are simply trying to win a contest.

Don't spend a great amount of time and energy in trying to "psych" an adversary. It is okay to be tricky, as in football or hockey. It is reprehensible to try to upset someone. Having seen and talked to many great athletes, I am always struck by their intense concentration. They focus on their *own* game, mental attitude and strategy. To do otherwise is to play a lesser game.

Years ago I played golf with a man who tried to throw off my game. Making comments that he thought would upset me, he said things like: "Boy, is this green fast." I paid no attention because I was thinking only about my game. What seemed like a fast green to him might be slow by my standards.

That man did very poorly that day—maybe because he spent too much time telling me what I should do. I didn't feel guilty about not ignoring him. Later on he admitted as much.

In conclusion, I believe that you enjoy more success if you learn to be comfortable with yourself. Let the other guy try all the manipulation or intimidation he wants. (That only shows he is worried about *you.*) Don't feel guilty about winning: you earned it fair and square. Anyone who has to win all the time is a born loser; he needs the win to save his ego. Somewhere, at the bot-

tom of his psyche, he feels the pangs of guilt and he
assumes you will, too. So show him you're different and
strip his defenses.

8

Guilt and Sexual Activity

Undoubtedly the most guilt-ridden area of our lives is that of dealing with sexual feelings and behavior. I believe there is more game playing with this activity than with any other form of human interaction. It is a most sensitive barometer as far as *personality integration* is concerned.

Early Life

Sexual manipulation by guilt starts in early childhood. Children soon learn taboo areas and sensitive subjects. The very young child often sees his parents frown when he touches his genitals. He reads signs of embarrassment in the faces of adults and consequently feels guilt and shame. He doesn't know exactly what he has done but he has clearly been offensive. And so the foundation of guilt is established.

Lack of verbal communication continues through later years, conveying a message indirectly: sex is so "bad" that you can't even talk about it. And so more guilt is added. Masturbation, a frequent activity in formative years, is another source of guilt. (Few adults are even comfortable with the word!) As a result, the child is manipulated into feeling guilty without clearly understanding just what is acceptable and what isn't. In the child's mind, anything sexual can bring on guilt.

The process accelerates during adolescence and the late teen years. Because there are rarely any discussions on the topic between adolescents and parents, the adolescent is left in a state of ignorance. He has no access to correct information nor any way to learn by the experiences of his older (and hopefully wiser) parents.

As a sex educator, I have seen this kind of situation many times; my wife Vi and I have taught classes on sex education for many years. Our emphasis is factual; we strictly avoid morality and do's and don'ts. We don't deny moral values but, instead, indicate that this area should be dealt with in the home. And we always have an initial meeting with the parents of the children we teach.

Many years ago we were asked to speak to a parents' group in a school that was considering hiring us. The school had never had a sex-education program before. Describing our program, we encountered much resistance from some parents. Viewing us as substitute parents, they wanted us to tell their children what *not* to do. We responded that we would discuss the dangers of promiscuity but would not force conclusions.

Finally, out of frustration, I invited the parents to propose a directive on what was acceptable. I informed them that one can't simply say: "No intercourse before marriage." Parents must spell out exactly what is permissable. Youngsters can't only rule *out* behavior; they must know specifically what is acceptable. For example if petting is discussed, then one must set exact guidlines-such as how far at what age; after how many dates; etc.

The parents couldn't handle this at all. A few of the more courageous ones stood up and presented their version of what was acceptable. As soon as they did this, however, others took exception. The discussion became more and more heated until it was finally clear that no definitive code could be established. There was an awful lot of emotion but no consensus. Therefore, I re-entered the discussion and indicated that what had transpired had provided a justification for our program's emphasis.

For many years Vi and I have had the privilege of teaching at another school where the atmosphere is

very different. Under the astute guidance of a fine principal, and an excellent PTA, the program facilitates
communication and inquiry. The youngsters learn basic
information in class and are then encouraged to ask
their parents for guidelines. The school is exceptionally
well run; obviously, the parents who have students
there want to do more than manipulate through guilt.
Which is a great start toward developing independent
minds!

Unfortunately, though, most adults find it difficult to
be this open. Since their own attitudes are heavily guilt-
laden, they generally transfer guilt to their children. As
a result the children learn manipulation by guilt, which
brings them in the front lines of the battle of the sexes.
Not only are many people unable to say no without
feeling guilty; many more can't say yes! If, in fact, few
people do much of anything but manipulate, what implications does this have past adolescence?

Normative Standards

I sometimes think that it's wrong for laypeople to read
studies of sexual behavior (Masters and Johnson et al),
because they don't know how to evaluate norms. Social
pressure for conformity encourages us to read the studies prescriptively. We have widely published norms
now, that tell how often the average person of a given
age does everything from masturbation to experiencing
orgasm. Many people infer that, if they don't measure
up, they are abnormal, undersexed, "queer" or God
knows what. They no longer ask themselves if they are
happy; they automatically feel guilty.

I recently counselled a young man who felt guilty because his various partners did not climax. He wondered
whether his foreplay was adequate; whether he unconsciously tried to punish women; whether he unconsciously selected "cold" women, and finally, whether
he reached orgasm too quickly. His first question was
how long should the sex act take. I said I never used a
stop watch! He told me he did, and averaged 3⅓ minutes. How could I compete with that?

I talked to him for a while and concluded that he was anxious, guilt-ridden, and too mechanical in his approach. I thought it might be helpful to speak to his girlfriend. (He had brought her along.)

As you'd imagine, she was also an overly guilt-ridden. She told me that her boyfriend kept asking her every 30 seconds if she had "released yet." "Could that be a problem?" she asked.

As a corrective, I suggested they try to relax more. Their homework was to not worry about the "great event," to develop their emotional relationship, and then to come back after a month. They didn't follow through, though. The boyfriend called two days later to announce that "everything is fine now." Maybe so—until next time when one of them feels guilty because of adequacy problems.

Recently I counselled a woman who said (for openers) that her sex life was great.

"Congratulations," I replied. "Then you must be here to discuss some other problem."

"No, Dr. Gunn. I am concerned about the sexual fantasies I have when my husband and I make love. They're different from the ones I've read about and I feel guilty because I must be "cheating my husband." Silently cursing the misguided source of her information, I persevered. (Later it occurred to me that the patient might have misread accurate information, but the result was the same.)

We talked for a while and I ascertained that she was loaded with guilt. Her mother had communicated the importance of honesty, loyalty, and (above all) "making your man first, last and always." That certainly gave me something to work with. We could see if her husband felt deprived. I scheduled a second appointment and asked her to bring her husband along. The result was similar to the other case mentioned previously. She called before her next appointment and said she was cancelling out. "*I* am willing to come but my husband isn't," she explained. He had said, "I am not going to any damn shrink to talk about my sex life. I like it just the way it is."

"Fine," I said, "Then it sounds like whatever you are

doing pleases your husband. Isn't that more important than anything you read in a book?''

''Oh yes, Dr. Gunn, and thank you so much.'' I wish that all such cases could be solved so easlly. People simply must learn to think for themselves and to judge what is right for them. I suppose that there is some value to norms because they give us a range of what people do. But, sexual behavior is highly individualized and a couple cannot bend themselves in order to approximate a norm. Behavior that isn't authenic seldom improves the quality of any relationship.

Premarital Sexuality

Premarital sex is especially vulnerable to manipulation by guilt. Let's identify the ''classical maneuvers'' utilized by men and women.

Males

First let's consider the sexually immature male. Classically, he believes that, in order to prove himself, he must be sexually active. Generally he does not believe he can be open with his girlfriend for various reasons. He may not want her to voluntarily submit to his advances—that would only diminish his conquest.

John D. was a case in point. A college student, he evidenced problems causing low grades. His study habits were poor. On those rare occasions when he did sit down to study, his mind wandered terribly. His manner was overly agressive (as I found out when I shook his hand).

Underneath the bravado, John was really ''milque toast.'' Loaded with insecurity, he was afraid of women and jealous of most men. He told me he constantly and compulsively thought about girls and sex. His goal was to ''lay waste to all the virgins on campus.'' Often he felt angry when he encountered a woman who had prior experience.

His seduction routine was to complain at length on the first date that college co-eds at his alma mater are "inhibited prudes." After he wined and dined his date, he'd suggest that she "owed" him a favor. If she didn't consent he would play the hurt little boy. (It was quite a lengthy routine.) When he was finally successful, he would act as if his companion had done something very wrong. He wanted her to feel guilty because that made *him* feel important. When he did succeed, the girl was twice manipulated. First, into bed, and then, into feeling guilty!

Bob G. was another sexual manipulator who didn't discuss his true feelings with his girlfriends. His double standard wouldn't let him. It was fine for men to have sexual feelings but not girls: girls who had sex were whores. To get his way, he would talk about how he needed a "sexual outlet," how all the "other girls are doing it," etc. As soon as the act was over, the relationship crumbled. The girl felt "used" and Bob could not consider dating a "whore."

The "prove you love me" concept has many serious drawbacks. Terribly one-sided, it always breeds resentment. Bob couldn't sustain a relationship with a girl for very long. If she didn't submit, he dropped her. If she did, he also ended the relationship because she was now a whore.

Clearly, young men who use this approach need to take a good look at themselves. They are bound to have problems when they do marry because they don't know how to share. Their sexual life usually tapers off after marriage. Furthermore, they can never enjoy friendships with women—which hampers both sexual and platonic relationships. Their characteristic manipulation will finally produce feelings of resentment and dependency.

It is, however, a law of sexual behavior that every response occasions a counter response. A game played by one sex is matched by a game played by the opposite sex. Sooner or later the two get together and then struggle to see who can out manipulate the other. Let's look at some female maneuvers.

Females

Janice characteristically felt guilty about her sexual impulses. She had been reared to feel she had something that boys wanted. But she couldn't give "it" to them. Girls are not supposed to have sexual feelings—at least "nice girls" aren't.

At 21, Janice couldn't take responsibility for her sexual feelings; she could only have sex if she was free of moral responsibility for what happened. Fortunately, she was quite ingenious at this game.

One trick was to go to a party and get drunk. After the liquor took effect, she would advertise her availabity. She would play up to one of the boys, act seductively and let everyone know that she was out-of-control due to the liquor. Sometimes she would even giggle and announce that she didn't know how she was going to get home.

Of course, there was always some young man that would oblige. The following morning, she would wake up next to someone she barely knew. Then she would manipulate the man into feeling guilty because he had "taken advantage of her." She wasn't responsible because she had been drunk. The man would absorb all the guilt and Janice didn't have to acknowledge that she had got what she really wanted.

However, in all likelihood both parties were losers. Since Janice couldn't really say "yes," she couldn't fully participate. She was not able to enjoy herself because she wasn't involved on an adult level. In addition, she always had to punish *herself* for her behavior. Sex had to be dangerous, therefore she failed to use contraception. The men were often unconcerned and didn't use any protection, so ultimately Janice got pregnant.

Mary was another woman who used sexual manipulation. She always pretended to be unwilling but managed to surrender in the end. Then her partner was made to feel that he had really conned her. To relieve his guilt he dated her for a time. Mary was skillful at suggesting that there might be a repeat performance if she was taken to some place special.

Obviously, deception doesn't enhance the quality of sexual response. All the spontaneity, joy and authentic emotion are sacrificed to appearances. Using manipulation contributes to a very neurotic relationship where sex is used to express anger rather than love. As a rule, don't indulge until consent is mutual and freely given—and only when you think it will strengthen the relationship.

Acting Out a Parental Wish

Many young people become sexually involved because of the mixed messages that stem from parents. This is much more widespread than is commonly realized. Generally it occurs when a parent isn't free to do his own thing. He has to live through a son or daughter and can actually make his children feel guilty if they aren't sexually active.

Janice, whom I spoke of earlier, was a case in point. Her mother was a rather frigid, guilt-ridden woman who gave Janice double messages about behavior. Sex was wrong for girls, but mother still wanted to hear about every experience. The tip-off was that mother had to hear every embarrassing detail.

Woodrow M. used the same approach with his son Woodrow Jr. was told that it wasn't nice to entice desirable young women in to bed but he made the practice sound so attractive that the son was interested anyway. Then he made the younger man feel guilty when he wasn't successful and when he didn't tell all the details to dad.

This double-message bind is very destructive because the youngster is punished in two ways. The son or daughter becomes involved out of someone else's need. I have advised many parents to try to be more guilt-free themselves, suggesting to their children that they not bother coming back.

Marital Sexual Manipulation

Marital manipulation begins even before the wedding. I realize that I run the risk of being called a male chauvinist, but I believe that girls manipulate more to get married than boys.

If I haven't lost readers by now, let me explain why. In our society there is more pressure for girls to get married than for boys. From early childhood, little boys seldom talk about being fathers; little girls are programmed to be mothers. The whole society manipulates the girl—particularly her parents. When boys manipulate, on the other hand, it is generally to cement a sexual relationship.

I have seen only one case like this. As it happened, the young man had been the woman's first lover. After they had been lovers for some time, he tried to make her feel guilty by suggesting they had done something very wrong. He suggested marriage was the answer. However, the girl apparently felt differently, and she turned him down.

As I said earlier, I have seen many young men who, by their own accounts, deliberately got girlfriends pregnant to marry them. Guilt was the weapon; hostility was the motivation. If a woman is responsible for her own birth control, she can avoid this bind. Unfortunately, most young women are too impulsive to take this precaution. For them, early sexual involvement is especially dangerous.

Women typically use three classic types of manipulation to get married. One is typified by Susie. She led Mike on for over a year, allowing and even initiating very heavy necking and petting sessions. Whenever he tried to persuade her to go further, she made him feel guilty.

"How could you ask me to do a thing like that before we get married? I'm just not that type of girl." Her comments made Mike feel guilty. Sometimes during their amatory sessions, Susie would breathlessly say, "Oh, Mike, I want you so, I hurt; I wish we were married!"

Comment like that made Mike feel he must be very sexy: he was driving Susie crazy with desire. After a few more build-ups, he asked Susie to marry him. She accepted immediately. As Mike soon learned, marriage didn't really change anything. Susie went right on with her manipulations.

Janet used a similar approach with Bill except that she finally "gave in"—an action she had planned all along. The relationship had been characterized by struggle. Bill was the hunter; Janet was the catch. Actually, she manipulated Bill so things only seemed that way.

Finally the big night arrived. Bill pushed for sex and this time Janet capitulated. Finally, after she had extracted sufficient commitment from Bill, she gave in—but only after he reassured her that he had never loved anyone as he did her. He also had to predict the future, promising that he never would love anyone that much—ever.

After the big event (which, incidentally wasn't all that great by both parties' admission) Janet began to have "guilt feelings." At least that's what she told Bill. She reminded him of her guilt feelings day after day but she still teased and "submitted" to lovemaking.

Gradually her point was clear. Bill felt like a heel. He had "taken" something from a sweet girl. She was not "that kind of girl," but she had succumbed to his pushiness. Now what could he do to make it up to her? Not surprisingly, Janet had the answer. So they were married and Bill always wondered how it had happened.

Needless to say, none of these approaches is likely to set a foundation for a good marriage. What is set up, instead, is dependency, guilt and so-called forced giving. No one should take something that another person doesn't want to give. If giving is mutual, fine. A marriage established on guilt continues along those lines. A marriage built on mutual sharing, however is conducive to growth and development.

Sexual Bargaining

After marriage, many kinds of sexual manipulations take place. For instance, one wife would wear her most seductive negligee on nights when she had reason to be tired. Frequently it would be the evening of the day that she had cleaned the entire house. As expected, her husband would approach her for relations: she would then talk about how tired she was. But she never put him off entirely. Instead, she would play her game and then finally give in. Now she had really done him a "favor."

That, of course, left him defenseless and he was often reminded of it until he made it up to her, such as when he brought her some new article of clothing. That was the pattern that was followed for years. When I suggested the couple select other nights for their love making, it was actually the wife who argued against that move.

I spoke earlier of Susie, who had manipulated Mike into marriage. Mike was sure that his guilt feelings would subside once the couple was married. In his mind, he would no longer feel obligation. Little did he realize that his guilt "trips" were only beginning.

Marriage manipulated him in new ways. Susie "loved him," found him "terribly appealing," but she just couldn't make love when she was "worried."

"About what?" Mike would reply on cue like a sucker. "Oh it's nothing, honey, but . . . well, the bedroom looks so messy. I guess I just can't relax in this room until we get our wallpaper up."

Mike should have suggested they try the garage, but no doubt something would have "bothered" Susie there too. Instead, Susie always gave in and that got her the wallpaper and everything else. I always suspected she decorated the whole house that way.

Mac used a similar technique on Julie, withholding sexual love and affection after every fight. The trouble was that the fights always took place after one of his many nights on the town. Mac was a successful salesman who would often stay out nearly all night without calling home. He liked his freedom and used the excuse that he had to wine and dine customers in order to sell insurance policies.

When he finally did come home, Julie was very upset. She wondered why he hadn't called; she was worried. She wanted him to hold her and tell her that he still loved her. Mac would always insist that he didn't feel "lovable" when a fight was in the making. Julie didn't want to lose him so she relented and the whole process was subsequently repeated.

Julie and Mac had a very stormy marriage in other ways. Julie had come from a broken home and had always felt bitterly rejected by her father. There had been a history of marital conflict in Julie's family. Her father had said many times that he would leave if he didn't have the children. He had always *seemed* very close to his son and daughter: he took them many places, spending a good deal of time playing with them when they were small.

At the same time, he continually complained that his wife was "cold," that she provoked fights, and that arguments erupted when he tried to talk to her. Julie always remembered her father as having much greater warmth than her mother. In retrospect, her mother had seemed dependent on the daughter; she often talked to her about her marital problems, crying as she talked. Julie grew up remembering her mother's word that "you are all I have."

When Julie entered her teens, there was a quick divorce. Julie stayed with her mother while her brother Bob went with her dad. Julie was bitterly disappointed and felt that, because Bob was a boy, he had special consideration. He could select the parent with whom he wanted to live while Julie had no such choice.

Life was even harsher to Julie in later years. A noteworthy incident occurred when she was just 13. Her father was transferred across the country; for Julie, the move meant she almost never saw him. At the same time her mother relaxed her grip on Julie. It was the age-old struggle of a parent being dependent upon a child. The child is then blocked in her natural development process. She is held back and conflict arises when she takes a step forward.

Manipulation by guilt followed every step of the way. When Julie's breasts began to develop, her mother seemed angry. She forced Julie to wear clothes that concealed her growing contours. When Julie began to menstruate, her mother was *clearly* angry. "Now you had better keep away from boys, young lady," was her mother's constant outcry. In addition, there were fearsome cross-examination periods after every party that Julie attended. When she was finally allowed to date at age 17, things got even worse.

There was one key fight that Julie recalled years later in therapy. Her mother had been unreasonably angry because Julie had talked to a boy who had a reputation for being fast. (Because he was a strikingly handsome, confident boy, he may have been saddled unfairly with that reputation.) Now, Julie already felt guilty because she had a good figure and had begun to menstruate. (Her mother had seen to that.) But she now had to feel guilty for simply talking to a boy. With this fight, Julie finally lost her temper.

"You want me to be as cold as you are, Mother," she shouted.

"You slut," her mother replied, slapping her.

Julie had come to feel that, perhaps, she was a lot like her mother. How could she help it? She felt guilt and anxiety about being womanly. She carried the memories of her father telling her mother that she was frigid. In addition, subconsciously Julie felt that if *she* had been more womanly, maybe her father might have stayed. That is a child's way of thinking that unfortunately endures.

So Julie carried these feelings into marriage. When her husband, Mac, stayed out late, she thought that, perhaps like her father, he wouldn't return. When he finally did return, she thought, "Now I have to turn on the warmth to keep him." Julie would make an advance and Mac would pull away. That was his way of making her feel guilty so she could not object to his nocturnal behavior. The rejection worked because Julie already felt guilty that she must not be sexy enough to keep Mac home.

Julie's situation did not improve until she had been in therapy for over a year, when she gradually began to see lovemaking as something that produced joy and brought people closer. She refused to play the game anymore. Mac ultimately went into therapy and showed some very significant improvement as well. The couple began to experience sexual fulfillment in a relationship free from manipulation. As these experiences suggest in sexual matters, manipulative game-playing never scores any points.

Sexual Experimentation

Since no two people are exactly alike, it stands to reason that everyone has different preferences in lovemaking. One partner may find some activity pleasurable that the other doesn't.

I saw a couple several years ago that illustrated this point. Jon enjoyed oral sex but his wife found fellatio unpleasant. There were constant fights about his wife's reluctance to perform this act. Jon would insistently allude to encounters with other sexual partners, insinuating how sexually "uninhibited" they were. Feeling guilty, his wife Jean would generally yield to his desires.

With Jill and Hank, the situation was reversed; Jill enjoyed oral sex (cunnilingus) while her husband didn't. To manipulate Hank, Jill would complain about feeling "unsatisfied" and imply that her husband was an awkward lover. Hank would submit to Jill's intimidation and subsequently would feel weak and inadequate.

I have seen many other examples of this abuse. As far as I can see, everyone loses in this kind of struggle. The victim of manipulation feels dominated and is a reluctant lover.

There are various approaches that can be used to remedy this unhappy situation. I suggest that a complete discussion take place in which both partners try to understand their mate's feelings. Many marriage counselors believe that a partner will be receptive to different techniques if properly introduced. I am not sure that I agree; individual preferences still exist. Instead, I feel that human beings are flexible and can generally work out their differences. It is usually possible to make adjustments and to compromise. It is better to have a substitute than to coerce a partner and end up with hositility. I believe that only the very immature can find just one way of achieving sexual gratification.

Sexual Manipulation by Jealousy

Jealousy can be used in many situations to produce guilt; it can also incite many other feelings. Jealousy can cause anger, competitiveness, anxiety, depression, etc. Since this book deals only with guilt I will necessarily limit my discussion.

One jealousy situation involves spouses who complain that they do not get all of the sexual attention they want. Walker was such a man, and his wife Nancy listened to more than her share of complaints. She got to the point where these complaints had little effect upon her. Walker realized this and changed his approach. He implied that perhaps Nancy no longer found him attractive. Maybe he was "over the hill" and no one would find him "sexy."

Nancy noticed that after a few such comments Walker's behavior at parties began to change. When he had always been shy, he began to be seductive and suggestive with other men's wives. This met with an interested reaction because many of these wives were trying to prove themselves too. The sexual joking continued back and forth and increased in magnitude. Walker would "joke" that he "couldn't get much action at home; I guess Nancy doesn't find me sexy."

The women "joked" back in the same way, saying that their husbands had been neglectful lately. One woman, Sheryl, made numerous comments about her husband's age and how this seemed to have lessened his prowess. More and more suggestive rewards were exchanged between Sheryl and Walker, and both of their spouses began to take notice. Sheryl's husband, Harold, began to become tense when the two couples met.

So the behavior of Walker closely paralled the behavior of Sheryl. He had started it, but Sheryl was glad
to use it on her husband as well. Walker took every opportunity he could to let Nancy see how attracted Sheryl was to him. If she was that attracted, why wasn't
Nancy?

Sheryl was using the same approach to get to Harold.

"Was he too old to respond like Walter did?" she
wanted to know. There were numerous comments to
the effect that it did her ego good to see that at least
one man found her attractive.

As I mentioned earlier, other emotions were aroused
by this behavior. Both Nancy and Harold felt angry at
their mates. In addition, they began to feel guilty. Harold asked himself many times if perhaps he didn't give
Sheryl all of the attention that a wife needs. Both Nancy and Harold became manipulated and became more
involved than they wanted. Sheryl and Walker did get
more "action" but they strained their marriages in the
process.

This kind of behavior deserves comment, but before
doing so I want to mention Jennie, a very guilt-ridden
girl who was also manipulative. Constantly flirting with
every man available at parties, she was sufficiently attractive to get some reactions. The flirting would ultimately produce some sort of proposition and Jennie
would persist until she had a firm offer.

At that point she would become frightened and filled
with guilt. Frequently she would directly blame the man
who had responded. It made no difference, though, because her sequence of actions was always the same.
She would go and confess to her husband. That way
her guilt reaction was reduced by the confession. In addition, she was subtly telling her husband that other
men found her attractive.

What can a husband do in a situation such as that?
He can't punish a wife for honesty. He is likely to be
forgiving and also much more attentive.

So the question is, what do all of these people—
Walker, Sheryl, and Jennie—get out of their behavior?
Very often they do seem to get what they want. They

have manipulated a spouse into feeling inadequate and guilty. As a result that partner may for a time become more attentive, sexually active, or whatever.

In the final analysis, though, everyone becomes a loser. When sexual activity is forced through manipulation, they are unlikely to respond well. Anxiety badly limits a person's ability to perform sexually. When that happens, nothing is much fun any more. Guilt also causes a reaction of anger and rebellion. Guilt-ridden people become angry at those who either caused or facilitated the guilt.

Of the people mentioned, Nancy was the only one from whom I later heard. She did rebel in a rather classic way. She let Walker know that if he wanted more action, he could find it right at home. She became very sexually aggressive and demanding. No matter what Walker did, she always wanted more. Walker ultimately began to have problems and discontinued his jealous approach.

My own feeling is that people are unwise to take their marital problems elsewhere. These difficulties need to be worked out within the marriage. The partner who refuses to be manipulated but requests a discussion is heading in the right direction. After all, the marriage is still the primary relationship; all efforts should be directed there. Hopefully, the victim will confront the manipulator. If so then marriages will become stronger. At least, we can hope.

Hostility

Unfortunately there is a great deal of hostility centered in marriage. No two people can ever live together without some outbreak of anger. Anger is not alarming if it is handled directly. It does create problems when it is expressed through sexual behavior. It then becomes another form of manipulation by guilt.

For example, Barbara had never been able to recognize, accept, and talk about her anger. Neither of her parents ever allowed that; her personality became set along those lines. Whenever she did get angry, she passively punished those around her by making them feel that they had failed her. When she married David she continued right along the same lines.

David was a reasonably secure man who was financially successful. As such it was difficult to make him feel a failure, but Barbara gradually began to find some chinks in the armor. She had accidentally hurried him while they were making love one evening and her behavior seemed to disturb his performance.

Unconsciously, that became Barbara's approach whenever she was angry at David. She would claim that she was "just so ready to go;" why wasn't he? David did not perceive the hostility because he was concentrating so fully on his unsatisfactory performance. He began to apologize for his failures, and his faith in his masculinity began to ebb.

David could never understand what accounted for his inconsistent sexual performance. He only knew it had something to do with marital conflicts. Barbara treated him more supportively when she wasn't angry. When she was angry, she would diminish him by referring to "his problem."

Unfortunately it becomes difficult to turn a partner on and off at will. With guilt comes large doses of anxiety and then increasing deterioration of one's sexual performance. David had increasing impotency which was accompanied by anxiety. As he lost self-confidence in one area of his life, he also suffered insecurities in other areas. David became depressed, and finally he was even less effective at the office. At that point he finally sought help; fortunately, his therapist immediately realized that Barbara needed help, too.

Because neither Tom nor Diane ever sought help with their problems, their continual conflict helped destroy their lives. Tom was a man with very poor control and an overabundance of anger. Many would say that he had the "only child syndrome"—he seemed to think of no one but himself. He had a very sharp tongue which he used constantly. Everyone wondered why someone didn't punch him out, but perhaps that was because people fled his company as fast as they could.

Tom always acted as if he was a very self-assured, fun-loving, free person. In fact, though, he was plagued by terrible feelings of insecurity. When half drunk he once admitted he had wanted to become a famous athlete. He had been on the high school football team for three years but played for a total of seven minutes in games.

Tom used to love to brag about how everyone was out to "lay the head cheerleader," but he had been the only "one to make it." The fact was, as he had confessed on another drunken occasion, that he had gotten the chance with this girl only accidentally. He had caught her on a rebound, when her boyfriend, the football captain, had dropped her. However, as Tom put it, he hadn't been "able to get it up."

Diane had been over-awed by Tom from the first moment they met. She fell for his big line and bravado. She saw him as a good catch—a man bound to get ahead. Diane couldn't believe that such a "bright" man would pay so much attention to her. There had not been many men that did pay attention to Diane in her early years. She had been quite sheltered by her mother and had become so shy that she didn't know how to respond to men when they did ask her out.

Tom probably felt secure with Diane because she was shy and inexperienced. He had publically bragged no man had laid a hand on her before him. Such an inexperienced girl was unable to see through Tom's sham bravado.

So for a few months of marriage things seemed to go well. Tom's ego was propped up because Diane was always so submissive and yielding to him. Diane felt important just being married to Tom.

The honeymoon ended very quickly, however. Tom felt that he had "created" Diane as far as sex was concerned. "I taught her everything she knows," he would often comment. How natural, then, that he would also attack his "creation's" sexual performance. When he became angry with her, he would tell her that she was a "lousy lay." Then he began to tell her that with a lover like him, she should be able to reach at least two orgasms during each love making session.

It is important to note that only when he was angry
was Tom was concerned about his wife's performance.
Her orgasm was important to him only as an ego trip
and as an attacking point. Diane didn't read Tom that
way, however. She felt that he must be genuinely concerned that she be fulfilled. She became more and
more guilt-ridden. Gradually sexual interaction became
a testing ground.

As Diane felt increasingly battered, she turned to alcohol. That impaired *all* of her functioning and she then
became the total target for Tom's hostility. She gradually lost all of her confidence and felt guilty for hanging
onto such a "good man." When she began to find evidence that Tom was seeing other women, her world to-
tally fell apart. At the age of 25, she died from a mixture of alcohol and sleeping pills.

The case of Tom and Diane is especially tragic because of the loss of her young life. However, all
couples who manipulate sexually to produce guilt and
thereby punish their mates are losers. Sexual love
should be joyful and conducive to emotional growth.
When anger becomes the prime factor, human relationships deteriorate. It would surely be a step in the right
direction if couples would attempt to talk out their anger and try to make sexual love fun. It's much more rewarding.

Manipulation for More Sex

The act of causing a partner to feel guilty because of a
low frequency of sexual relations seems much more
prevalent among men than women. At least my professional experience bears this out. There may be many
reasons for this but I won't go into them here.

I will say that with the change in women's behavior,
there are certainly more women today who push ag-
gressively for sex. I have recently seen two women who
were able to manipulate.

They have very similar personalities; basically their
approach lacks complexity. They approach their men

repeatedly. If turned down several times, they consequently talk about it. Usually they ask their men whether they don't find them attractive anymore. They soon get a response because their men don't want to admit that they can't keep up with their wive's sexual desires.

In other words, it only takes a small amount of manipulation to make the man respond. I doubt that guilt plays a large part, but it would appear that it is a factor. Men are so afraid of being considered inadequate lovers that they quickly respond. Anxiety seems higher if they refuse the women's request than if they assent. As one man said, "I may not be able to make it but I will sure die trying."

On the other hand, though, I have heard many reports that men manipulate in a variety of ways to increase sexual frequency. The examples I provide represent a common occurence.

My first illustration involves a couple—Ron and Helen. They had been married nine years when they first applied for marital counseling. Helen's complaints were varied: she had a high level of guilt and anxiety and felt that there were too many pointless quarrels. On the other hand, Ron felt there was too little sexual activity.

As far as their sex life went, Ron was a score keeper. Each night that they did not make love, he would note this fact. The next evening, he would approach Helen again with the comment: "I thought maybe you would be in the mood because it's now been 11 days." If Helen said no, then Ron added a day to the tally.

Always anxious and guilt-ridden, Helen felt increasingly ill at ease. She hated the approach but sooner or later, despite her mood, conceded. But she would get back at Ron for making her feel guilty. She soon grew to hate sex as her discomfort increased year by year. This couple seemed ready for the divorce courts by the time they came for help.

Another husband, Kevin, used virtually the same approach on his wife Julie. The only difference was that he circled the days on the calender when they made love and quoted frequency tables to his wife. A woman who made love only once a week was half as feminine as a woman who was willing to have sex twice a week.

Julie began to feel increasingly unfeminine as her performance slacked off. She felt indicted as a bad wife and a "cold woman." Julie tried to make it up to Kevin by doing more and more things for him. He never seemed to feel satisfied with any of her efforts. The only thing that counted was how many nights she said yes.

So Julie, pushed by her guilt feelings, began to say yes more often, regardless of how she felt. Kevin was pleased with her acquiescence but criticized her because she didn't achieve the average number of orgasms. Gradually Julie began to lose faith in herself and lost pleasure in lovemaking. This too offended Kevin's ego. A woman had to perform as he saw it and she *had* to enjoy it. Otherwise it negatively reflected upon his masculinity.

Finally, Julie was too anxious to enjoy sex at all. She became so tense that intercourse was painful. Then of course, she became very resistant, Kevin began to manipulate again by noting the drop in frequency.

Julie began to feel that she just couldn't make it in marriage, and for a time the couple was close to divorce. Julie did not want to end the marriage and ultimately persuaded Kevin to go to a local clinic for marital counseling.

The couple was involved in counselling for nearly two years. Julie responded well; her guilt and anxiety level dropped. She felt that a new freedom defined her sexual performance.

Kevin found it difficult, however, to modify his behavior. Manipulation by guilt had worked so well he couldn't see anything wrong with his approach. When he finally did change, the couple developed a very sound and constructive marriage. They seemed to have fun together and lovemaking was joyful. Quite naturally the frequency of relations increased, but the main improvement was in the quality.

I recognize that manipulation through guilt may for a time increase the frequency of intercourse, but it will always harm relations in the long run. I don't feel anyone should be coerced into intimacy. It isn't fair and limits everyone's enjoyment.

In addition, I don't feel that the manipulative approach will work for long. Remember that people who feel guilt punish others for their guilt feelings. Sooner or later the one manipulated will rebel and will deny their partner sexual relations. I have talked to many wives who have told me they say no even when they wanted to say yes. This was their habitual response to sex and manipulation.

The best way to increase frequency is to increase the pleasure. You can accomplish this by removing feelings of guilt, anxiety, and pressure. Instill an atmosphere of relaxation, warmth, and joy. Make sexual experience a time of joy and sharing. Chances are there will be more lovemaking. After all, people do make a habit of doing things that are fun.

Extramarital Affairs and Guilt

Surprising as it may sound, there are those who enter into affairs because of guilt feelings. Those who are guilt-ridden may find the clandestine affair less guilt-producing. It seems related to the secrecy factor. Many people I have seen who were never given permission by their parents to be sexually experienced felt marital guilt over sex. Curiously, they did not report guilt feelings with their affairs.

Guilt reactions may also provide another motive for an extramarital relationship. Some people become angry at themselves because of their guilt feelings. They feel that they are passive and restricted. As a result they rebel and plunge into the "forbidden" activity.

The extramarital affair, however, is often fraught with manipulation by guilt. I saw a woman, Betty M., who was a prime manipulator. She was highly skilled at finding men who would easily succumb to their guilt feelings.

Betty would first start talking to a man about how bad her home situation was. She described herself as a "warm woman," but said her husband wouldn't come near her for weeks on end. She "needed" physical love, "but what can a girl do, most men are afraid to respond to a sex-starved girl?"

That, of course, brought the desired response. The new target must prove his manhood through infidelity. He would feel guilty otherwise. In addition, here is a girl asking for something that he believes he can give. It becomes doubly difficult to say no.

Unfortunately, as soon as the man makes an overture, Betty would waver. She declared that she found him "terribly stimulating" but she would feel guilty cheating on her husband. Betty then adds that she doesn't want to be "just another lay" for a guy only looking for a good time.

Now the trap is baited and set. When the man gets involved (and most did) he finds a very dependent, guilt-ridden woman. He must constantly reassure her; must help her deal with her guilt; and must constantly tell her that she is more than just "a lay" to him. The man finds himself manipulated into a very dependent relationship. When he can no longer provide all the attention Betty needs, she ends the affair and looks for someone new.

Bart was a man who was also generally on the prowl; furthermore, he had constant conflict with everyone around him. He had a habit of finding guilt-ridden girls who could be talked into an excursion outside of marriage. Bart needed these affairs to prove to himself he was still attractive. He generally went after shy girls who resisted for a time and then gave in. The pursuit was the rewarding part of the contest for Bart.

Generally the girls felt very guilt-ridden afterwards. They generally blamed Bart for their guilt and managed to do something "careless" so that his wife found out. They also confessed their affairs to their husbands, which certainly failed to enhance Bart's popularity.

I advise anyone who is thinking of getting involved outside the marriage to take a good look at their motivation first. If you are trying to escape from guilt reactions in your marriage, you will find even more guilt in outside affairs.

9

Guilt And Marital Interaction

If I had to select one area in which guilt is prevalent, it would be in marriage. I sometimes wonder if it isn't almost entirely built upon this negative emotion. As long as this prevails, I don't believe marriages can be happy.

Of course, it is probably true that guilt manipulated many people into marriage in the first place. Two examples, seen thousands of times by all kinds of counselors, can illustrate this point. Let us look at what many men do first.

Before Marriage

John J. started dating Sylvia G. when they were both in high school; he was a senior; she was a junior. John was always described as shy and backward where girls were concerned. He was really very good looking and as a result girls often teased him. Since he had no excuses for not responding, his reticence was that much more conspicuous. John liked girls but he couldn't get up the nerve to make the first move. Boys kidded him about being afraid of girls, of being queer, etc. All of this pushed him further into a shell.

Quite by accident, he met Sylvia and was able to share some mutual interests with her. He began to feel wanted and slowly got up the nerve to ask her out. To his surprise, she accepted. Their first date was seeing a movie; John felt relaxed because he didn't have to talk. He had a nice time and later asked her what she was doing the following night.

Sylvia had enjoyed the movie and did not find John unpleasant. She had dated other boys and was generally a popular girl, but when she broke up with her steady, she found herself out of circulation. John's persistent method of asking her out was hard to refuse. She recalled later that if he had asked if she wanted to go out on another date the following night, she might have refused.

But he didn't. When she couldn't come up with definite plans for that evening, he had pushed. Feeling a little awkward, she had found it easier to accept.

One date followed another and changes began to take place with John. He began to talk as he had never talked to a girl before. He confessed that he never felt comfortable around girls before and, of course, Sylvia was flattered. John even told her how happy his overly-protective mother was that he was dating. Sylvia did not at first see how dependent John was becoming upon her. Anytime he felt depressed or insecure, he called her to talk about it.

It was clear John felt happier with Sylvia; he needed to pour his troubles out to someone. At times she tired of his complaints but felt guilty when she told him so. In fact, she felt guilty when she didn't encourage him to talk about how "badly he had been treated."

Sylvia was clearly much more outgoing than John— she mixed better with people, and she preferred parties to constant solo dates. But she knew that John felt uncomfortable in large groups and so she infrequently asked to double or go to parties. As a result, John felt more and more secure with her. Since she was not honest about her feelings, he felt she liked being with only him.

The couple dated steadily during their last year of high school; then John left for college. She felt some odd measure of relief as she stayed home to attend a clerical college. However, John soon felt "lonely" at college and began returning home nearly every weekend. During the week Sylvia did occasionally go out on dates. After all, she was not going steady. John didn't say anything but it clearly hurt his feelings.

Feeling guilty about hurting John, Sylvia declined

more and more dates. As this happened, the relationship became more *mutually* dependent. Summer came and passed; the couple still dated exclusively.

After several years, John decided that it was time he made the relationship permanent. With little prior warning, he asked Sylvia to marry him. She was shocked at first—there had never been any talk of marriage. She wasn't sure she really loved John but somehow the relationship had become comfortable.

Somehow Sylvia did not feel comfortable about marrying John. At first she argued that although they spent a lot of time together, they really didn't know one another. They hadn't talked about their goals, dreams, or even family aspirations. John had many more years of school ahead of him: how would they manage?

John had one comment for every objection Sylvia raised. ''I only know I love you and I have never felt so comfortable with anyone before in my whole life. I don't think anyone else could make me happy.''

Now how do you argue with that? If John was in love, how could Sylvia be anything else? Surely she didn't want to ruin his whole life. Sylvia struggled with her doubts for several days, but in the end John won out. The couple was married and struggled for years in an unhappy marriage. Both were so guilt-ridden that they were afraid to mention their true feelings. What started in guilt continued in guilt.

Now let's look at how a woman manipulates. Fran began dating Bill in early high school days and quickly decided he would be a good catch. Her mind was made up that he was the *one*, she later admitted, on their second date. Bill at first dated a few other girls but Fran's quiet (and not so quiet) tears made that uncomfortable. So the couple dated exclusively until their junior year.

Then Fran began to push, subtly at first and then more overtly. All of her friends were going steady: she felt insecure in the relationship because there was no official understanding. I wonder whether she wanted an announcement in sky writing but she was working for Bill's class pin. She took every opportunity to admire it on Bill's sweater and was overly enthusiastic as she publicly congratulated her "pinned" girl friends. Bill began to feel more and more guilty. He was depriving Fran of happiness; he wasn't doing for his girl what other boys did for theirs.

At Christmas time, he spent much of his meager savings on a genuine cashmere sweater. That would make it up to Fran. Naturally, it didn't.

"It's nice, Bill. Of course, I just love it but I wish you hadn't spent so much money. I think you know what would really make me happy."

Fran's birthday came in April and her campaign stepped up as the date approached. There were unspecified periods of crying, frequent statements of how much she loved him, and jokes about what she knew he was going to give her.

Bill finally succumbed to the pressure of his guilt and gave Fran the pin as a birthday gift. Ecstatic, Fran immediately showed the pin to all of her girl friends. One might have expected Fran to rest on her laurels but she didn't. She told Bill in a giggly manner how many of her girl friends wondered if they were engaged. Bill just avoided that covert confrontation.

Bill had lofty plans about college but instead he was drafted into the army. His first year was spent at a camp close to home so he saw Fran frequently. His second year was spent far from home and the couple therefore seldom saw one another. Fran wrote five letters to every one that Bill wrote and often teasingly said maybe he had lost interest in her. She constantly reminded him of the many offers she had to go out, but she always refused these dates. Bill said it wasn't fair to tie her down but she insisted she wasn't asking anything of him; she couldn't look at another man.

Then Bill was discharged and returned home to search for a job. Suddenly Fran began complaining of her job—how she hated to think of a career at the office where she worked. Being a housewife for a man she loved was all she wanted. Bill avoided the hint but the guilt hit its mark.

Four months later, Fran sat down to have a serious talk with Bill. She wanted to have some sort of understanding. All of her friends were married or engaged:

she was embarrassed being the only single one. If Bill didn't want to marry her, she wanted to know. She couldn't look at another man, but if Bill didn't want her she would manage somehow.

Bill proposed and Fran accepted. In the spring, they were pronounced man and wife until . . . well, for as long as they could stand it.

See what manipulation by guilt achieves? It is unlikely that either of the couples will be very happy. They have made a choice—not upon reason or even romance, but out of manipulation. The excessive attention that John and Fran required gets to be a big burden after a time. The pumping up of someone's ego gets wearing after a while and finally the insecure or dependent person gets to be a heavy load to carry. Before we go on to the next phase, it seems worthwhile to talk about what should have been done.

People should never allow themselves to be manipulated into something as important as a marriage. If either partner feels uncomfortable, they should avoid saying "I do." Marriage should be built upon mutual needs, interests, goals, and physical attraction. You need to be friends with one another and to work for mutual growth. You simply cannot do that when you start the relationship off feeling sorry for an insecure, dependent person.

The reader might ask why a John and a Fran don't get married to one another. It is rare but it does happen. In this situation, you have two dependent people hanging on one another. Generally the insecure person looks for someone who will be manipulated into constantly offering support. Two equally insecure people aren't sufficiently strong to offer any support. They both ask to be supported in their strong dependency needs at the same time.

Now let us look at the second stage of the relationship and follow the natural progression of manipulation by guilt.

The Need for Attention

Sylvia soon found John's ego was not permanently
strengthened by the fact he had married the girl of his
dreams. He needed constant reassurance. This need
was presented in many ways. We will omit the sexual
area because it belongs in another chapter and because we can find many illustrations without it.

John was always concerned about how he looked. In
the morning when he began dressing, he complained
constantly about his appearance. He had nice clothes;
partially because he possessed good taste, and partially
because he always insisted Sylvia go shopping with
him. That was not enough; in the mornings, Sylvia had
to approve every article of clothing he put on. She
complained that she could barely get dressed herself in
time to get his breakfast.

"Okay, honey, I guess you don't care any more how
I look," John retorted to her protests.

That usually did it: the old guilt feelings returned.
Sylvia hung around long enough to match his outfits
and tell him how good he looked. In time she came to
hate morning, but other periods were equally wearing.
John never seemed to get enough praise.

John worried incessantly about his business acumen
and needed constant praise about that, too. When he
didn't get it, he complained that Sylvia didn't care if he
got ahead. Other wives helped their husbands. "I just
want to get ahead so you will be proud of me," he told
her. With that approach, what guilt-ridden wife could refuse to support her man?

Sometimes John would force Sylvia to make decisions for him. He accomplished this by telling her how
much he admired her mind. Then he sabotaged her advice, made it fail and reminded her of it. Either way,
she felt guilty.

Fran used similar tactics on Bill. She never had
enough clothes, even with a full closet.

"Why don't you go out and buy more clothes,
then?" Bill often asked in frustration.

No matter what he said or did, though Fran never
seemed to have enough clothes or the right kind. She

wanted to be an eye-stopper and was really looking to Bill to constantly tell her she was gorgeous. No matter how often Bill did that, though, it was not enough.

It is rare for manipulation by guilt to be entirely one-sided in any relationship. If one person uses this tactic, it is reciprocally used by the partner. This is particularly true in marriage. In the case of Bill and Fran one could see the two-way manipulation of intellectual pursuits. When Fran tried to become involved in Bill's business affairs, she was put off with the reminder she didn't know much about business. The struggle constantly continued, though. Fran sought attention in every area of the marriage.

As a result, there were days when Bill had trouble getting work done at the office. Fran would call because she was "lonesome," when Bill tried to shorten the conversation, there was conflict. "You don't find me interesting anymore," would be the charge. Then the reassuring had to start all over. Bill felt double-hinged guilt. Fran was hurt and he was taking time from his boss to deal with marital difficulties.

I could go on and on citing examples of the use of guilt for attention. I have seen more of the same in many other marriages. The question is, how do we handle this nagging problem? A basic rule of human interaction is to support that which you like and to offer no support to what is offensive. Set limits based upon what you can tolerate. Let us look at two cases for solutions.

John needed to be either more self-reliant or less dependent. Sylvia should have avoided being manipulated into doing things for him that he should have done for himself. For example, she could tell him an appropriate number of times that he looked nice in his clothes. She should not overdo it. She needed to express support in his ability to match his wardrobe by himself; she could teach him some basic rules and then let him put these principles into effect.

If she wanted to carry things a step further, she could give him all of the help dressing he wanted for a couple of times. Then his breakfast wouldn't be ready and he would have to either go without or help her get the breakfast ready.

She could also remind him that he was not a child (or supposedly not) and that she was not his mother. He had to learn to stand on his own feet. The same with business decisions: he can't be effective in business if he always relies upon her decision—making. A sharp boss will deem him too passive and indecisive.

The same holds true for Bill and Fran. She needs to learn to select her own clothes and to choose things that make her look good. Bill needed to give *adequate* reassurance but not too much. He could tell her he loved her but that he had to have privacy at the office because his work required it. Limits have to be set. In all cases, if these techniques don't work, there exist problems that require professional help.

Jealousy

Another problem that occurs in many marriages is the use of jealously to secure an end. Usually the aim of the manipulator is to gain more attention and to build up a sagging ego. By seeking attention outside of the marriage, one conveys the message that he is a well sought after commodity. Their partner had better pay closer attention. There is also the message that what is given is lacking in quality. "Others value me more than you do," is one such subtle statement. Likewise "you are spending too much time with someone else."

This is a very dangerous problem with which to deal, as everyone loses. I strongly suggest that a couple sit down and discuss their needs and define what the problem areas of their marriage are. It is best to check this problem right at the onset: excessive jealousy drives people further apart. Try to satisfy important needs within the marriage and attempt to be realistic in demands. Don't smother appropriate outside relationships. No two people are ever going to satisfy all of each other's needs.

Domination

Quite often, there is a struggle for a power within the marriage. John, for example, did not feel strong and competent. He was basically insecure and dependent but still wished to be powerful and controlling. Whenever Sylvia tried to do her own thing, John became competitive. However, he always managed to lose the competition to Sylvia. Then he would subtly make her feel guilty for besting him.

For instance, he made her feel guilty about the many times she wanted to go back to school. At first, there were arguments that she wouldn't be able to handle her wifely duties and still go to evening classes. When logic prevailed over that argument, John began to make little statements such as; "You will probably get better grades than I got."

When Sylvia finally did succeed in taking a few classes, she did do well. As a result, John sulked. She finally gave up because she felt so terribly guilt-ridden about her success. John was relieved because, as he put it, "A man needs to be the master of his own domain."

John's need to dominate Sylvia spilled into other areas as well. When the couple socialized with others, Sylvia had to play dumb. Once there had been a four-way discussion at a party about politics. It began as a pleasant exchange of views. (There was no need to get highly emotional because all four people held the same political views.) However, Sylvia proved to be better informed than John and that "made John feel inferior." Sylvia felt guilty and allowed John to continually interrupt her. Gradually she withdrew from the conversation. Even so, on the way home, John remarked that she had dominated the conversation.

Bill was experiencing a similar conflict with Fran. He received a whole bunch of what a psychologist calls "mixed messages." Fran wanted him to be successful: that would mean more money and more stylish clothes. She could then let her friends know that she was married to a very successful businessman. That told people she must be quite a woman.

However, when Bill was successful, she would make him feel guilty because he was "accomplishing more in life" than she was. If he appeared intelligent, then how could he be satisfied with "a plain Jane like me?" She tried to limit his areas of competency to the business world; of course, this meant she dominated him at home.

Bill wanted to be involved in their home life, too, but was seldom allowed to do so. If he tried to arrange the landscape or build shelves, Fran accused him of trying to take over. Clearly he was not allowed to make any decisions without protest. Fran would state outright that the house was hers to run. Naturally, she carried that view to the extreme; the home life *should* be shared. Fran manipulated Bill to the extent that he felt guilty about his activities around the house. He couldn't make suggestions about furniture; he couldn't change the yard around; and even repairs had to be done according to his wife's dictates. Even their social life was directed by Fran except for the business related aspect.

Sports was another area of conflict. Bill had been an excellent tennis player in school. Fran had always fancied an interest in the game. On occasion, she played a few games of mixed doubles with Bill and another couple. Bill and Fran always won because of Bill's skill and Fran found this disturbing. They eventually had to stop playing together. Fran complained Bill was so good that he dominated the game. When he let her return more of the shots, she still complained. He was "too good," and she didn't want to play a game where she came off second best. Refusing the lessons from the local professional which Bill offered to pay for, she made sure she never could improve her game.

Fran was good at bridge; better, in fact than Bill. Bill openly admitted that and admired her playing ability. He soon began to hate bridge, however, because Fran publically pointed out how "stupid his bidding" was. Gradually there became less and less that the two of them could do together.

People should have room in which to grow and develop their own skills. Security comes from within; the secure person doesn't need to destroy others around them. If the need to dominate destroys the growth of a mate (and it surely will), then a discussion is in order. The dominated person needs to remove his guilt, to support his partner's talents, but to declare that he needs to develop his own talents. No one can constantly live in the shadow of someone else. Support your mate, but demand if necessary that which is your own. There are sufficient hours in a day to allow everyone to meet the realistic needs of others and still have time for ourselves. Feeling self fulfillment, we will be better able to give to those around us.

Family Arguments

Every deeply involved couple will have their share of arguments. When people say that they have never had an argument, I always wonder whether it is because they aren't involved enough to care. Either that or one of the two is so dominated that he doesn't even fight back. Arguments can strengthen a marriage if communication takes place, viewpoints get exchanged and if the argument is above board.

When arguments are resolved by manipulation through guilt, very little, if anything, constructive takes place. One of the key techniques used in such manipulation might be called the "smoke screen." Let's look at two such examples.

One husband I saw, George W., used two types of smoke screens. He had once been told that he had slightly high blood pressure and he might develop some heart problems if his pressure were not reduced. The prediction was simply a caution; his condition was not felt to be dangerous at the present time. A diet had been prescribed and there was reasonably satisfactory reduction in blood pressure.

George had interpreted the doctor's comment to mean there was something alarmingly wrong with his heart. No amount of reclarification served to correct that impression.

Whenever there was a family argument (regardless of how trivial), he would grab his chest and imply that the

argument was causing him a heart attack. Sometimes
he would claim to be so upset that he could not continue the discussion. His wife would immediately become
concerned and back off. He persisted until she felt terrible guilt pangs about even initiating a discussion.

George had another ploy. He had been told by his
doctor to cut down on his work. A perfectionist who always found jobs to be done (whether at home or office), he made it clear that family discussions took time
away from work. When his wife did not immediately
bend to his wishes, he would say something to let her
know she was taking his time. Now he would have to
work late into the evening. Or he didn't have time to relax in front of the TV. What wife would run the risk of
causing her husband to have a heart attack?

For women, crying is an effective smoke screen.
Cheryl O. used that technique to perfection. She could
turn on a waterfall at a moment's notice. Then her husband would break down and apologize. Immediately,
the crying would cease.

Smoke screens obscure the real issue. Instead of
solving anything, the smoke screen diverts attention.
For example, I asked George's wife if there was any
correlation between his chest pains and his success in
the argument. She replied that she had never thought
of that before. Later she reported that he never complained of pain when he was winning. So the discussion
wasn't what hurt; it was the losing.

One can't work out problems that way. A problem
can only be solved by sticking to the central issue.
Anything that diverts attention is counter-productive. If
you sincerely wish to see problems solved don't allow
the smoke screen to be used. I suggested this to the
spouses of George and Cheryl. I instructed them to tell
their partners that it appears they are unable to continue the discussion at present. "You have something on
your mind that needs to be discussed; if it can't be
considered now, you will bring it up later when they are
composed."

If possible, it is always better to try to point out what
is going on. Maybe the other person is not aware of
what they are doing. The trick is to get them to see the

immaturity of their ways and to never allow the smoke screen to work. If they have any self-awareness, they will be able to develop more rational ways of dealing with conflict.

Marital Bargaining

Broadly speaking, this involves manipulating someone to do something they don't want to do by giving them something you don't really want to give. It is a "you owe me now," statement and an excellent bluff. People like that never really let go when they give: there are always strings that are attached. A case in point was Louise and Walter Smith. Walter absolutely hated yard work. He worked on a construction job and felt that he had sufficient physical activity at work. Louise was a meticulous person who wanted their yard to look like a well-manicured nursery. Walter went far towards meeting her needs; he hired two boys to come in for yard work three times a week.

Unfortunately, no one could satisfy Louise. The flower beds were less than perfect, so Louise insisted that every flower bed be hoed once or twice a week. Walter refused to yield even though the hired boys did not clean out "every single" weed. There was a stalemate for quite a long time.

Then Louise hit on a plan. The couple had their own swimming pool, which Walter took care of by himself. Enjoying this job, he regularly washed the deck, brushed off the algae within the pool and added the necessary chemicals. Suddenly, when Walter came home at night, be began to find Louise hard at work at the pool. She refused his help and usually timed her work so everything was near completion at about the time he returned home.

"I know how much you love your pool, honey," she would coo demurely, "and I just want it to be perfect for you."

Walter began to feel guilty; he did love the pool. While it was true he had always thought of it as *theirs*, he did admit that he used it more than she did. He wished she would let him do the pool work, but how could he tell her? Especially after all of her effort to please him.

He simply could not bring himself to do this and began to bend to the manipulation. Little by little, he spent less time in the pool he loved so much and more time doing the yard work that he hated. Walter never complained about the yardwork because Louise didn't complain about working on the pool for him. He wished he could have exchanged jobs but he knew Louise hated yardwork as much as he did.

The story of another couple by the name of Bob and Marie Jones illustrates how men manipulate through guilt. Bob wanted the house to be kept in an immaculate manner. His mother had been a fastidious housekeeper. Prior to marriage, Bob had claimed he didn't like that quality in his mother. He had often declared that home had not been fun because everything always had to be put away. He recalled how, as a child, toys had to be returned to their place as soon as one finished with them. He wasn't going to let his home be run that way. Marie was glad because that style didn't fit her set of habits either.

Things began to change, though shortly after the couple was married. Bob would comment that the beds were a little messy, or the floor was dusty, and so on. At first, Marie ignored those comments but gradually she began to feel annoyed. She mentioned her feelings to Bob and sometimes silenced him by saying that he sounded more and more like his mother.

After that point, Bob said very little about how Marie kept the house. Instead he would come home, complain about how tired he was and then start some cleaning project. He would walk around emptying ash trays or wastebaskets or even running the vacuum. Although he never complained about these chores, it was obvious from his facial expression that he hated doing them.

Eventually, Marie began to feel inadequate and guilty. She wanted Bob to be happy and she hated to see him doing housework. That was her job. In her mind, she was letting him down. Since he didn't overtly complain, she couldn't easily fight back. In time, she found herself scurrying around to clean the house before he came home. She actually tried to anticipate what he was going to correct when he came home. From her point of view the house was beginning to feel like a prison. In consequence she began hating all the work she had previously enjoyed.

Never allow anyone to give you something they do not actually want to give. If they insist on doing so, let them know that they are doing it of their own volition. As with most marital or interpersonal problems, try to get things out in the open. Discuss what your feelings are and acknowledge your limitations. Walter, for example, enjoyed working in the pool after a hot day working outside. Accordingly, he should have had that job. Finally, he hired workers to keep up the yard. If Louise is unhappy with the results, she can hire someone else, provide more adequate supervision, or do it herself. The same applies to Bob; no one is perfect. If he wants to try, let him. But make sure he knows, it was his decision.

Marriage is a matter of continual adjustments and compromises. When someone is forced by guilt to do something they don't like, they become unpleasant company. Each of us has a job to do and we should try to do it adequately. If someone else is dissatisfied, we may try to alter our approach but only within the limits of our personal integrity.

Alcoholism

This is a very complex behavior disorder generally caused by a number of different personality factors. However, there is usually much manipulation by guilt when alcoholism occurs within marriage. The alcoholic is generally a very dependent person who seeks attention from others. Frequently he is inclined to feel neglected.

At this point the drinking begins. His wife often gets angry with his behavior but feels sorry for him as he becomes helplessly drunk. She gradually is manipulated by guilt into taking care of him as if he were a baby. By doing this, she is reinforcing his behavior. Often she gets rewards from others for her great sacrifice.

The marital interaction involving alcoholism is very complicated and interwoven. In my experience it requires professional help to change it. I do not know of any short cuts.

Spending Money

Helen and Bart J. came for counseling because of a conflict over handling money. They had no idea what was happening between them but they were aware that it had to do with financial matters. At first, it looked like a simple matter of giving financial advice. As the couple talked to their counselor, however, deeper problems were evident.

There were simply too many "hidden messages" for anyone to be able to give practical advice. For example, Bart frequently said he didn't care how much money Helen spent as long as she spent it "wisely."

"I earn well over a $100,000 per year," he declared, "so we have plenty of money. Our home is paid for and we are free of debt. But I didn't get where I am by wasting money. I believe we all have to be thrifty!"

Now, that is what he said, but what he actually did was very different. He handled the family finances so that all expenses were carefully budgeted. Helen was told to just come to him whenever she wanted to buy something that wasn't budgeted. For example, she had a monthly clothing allowance. She could exceed it only with Bart's permission. Right away, one can see now she was placed in a difficult position. No one wants (or should want) to be that dependent.

In addition, Bart was an overly conscious spender. He didn't spend much on himself and he expected others to do likewise. When Helen did buy something, there was a discussion of the utility of the purchase. Bart would usually convince her that she had made an unwise purchase. She was such a guilt-ridden person that she was quick to concede that her purchase was foolish.

Helen's upbringing contributed to her guilt in financial matters. Helen came from a family which had very little money. It had been her mother, and not her father, who was stingy with money. For a long time, Helen had felt guilty over nearly any expenditure of money. For that reason, she subtly gave Bart messages that she wanted him to limit her purchases—at least those made strictly for herself.

It eventually became clear that we had a couple who played each other back and forth. Each used guilt with the other. Such intertwinings are difficult to unravel because of mixed desires. Bart wanted Helen to spend money and yet he didn't. Helen wanted freedom and yet she was afraid of it. Interactions like that usually do take counseling to correct. Where there is one clear-cut message though, there are some easier corrections.

Try to work out a family budget and attempt to communicate in such a way that everyone can express his needs. Obviously, essentials have to be considered first. After that, try to see that there is some spending money allotted for each family member. In this way a husband doesn't have to run to his wife, (nor she to him) for each little purchase. Major purchases should be decided jointly.

Compliments

We would generally think that compliments are constructive because they help make people feel secure and confident. Such is not always the case. Compliments can be used as an insidious form of manipulation by guilt. As common sense tells us, a compliment is one method of stamping our approval upon someone else's action.

For example, I counselled one man who constantly praised his wife for being poised, lady like and sedate. His wife, Joan, had a mother who was subtly dominating with her children, but presented a facade of being outwardly quiet, withdrawn, passive, and lacking in spontaneity. In consequence Joan had much resentment for her mother. As a child, Joan was never allowed to show enthusiasm. Her mother always said with sharpness, "Joan dear, act like a lady." Joan struggled for many years to change her personality. She loved sports (forbidden to her as a girl), learned to have opinions and worked at being assertive. Ironically she married a man who reincarnated her mother's influence.

Or look at the case of Sam: he wanted to be more aggressive. His wife feared aggressive men because her father had been abusive to both her and her mother. She grew into womanhood disliking any show of aggressiveness. So she married a somewhat passive man and then by selective praise, tried to keep him that way.

Or take Dora as an example. She had been reared to believe that women should be beautiful and dumb. It was deemed unwomanly to have an opinion or an intellect. Internal conflict simply had to develop because, with a measured IQ of 138, she was anything but dumb. The trouble was, she married a man who was very much like her parents. Her husband admired her beauty and gave her constant attention for it, but never said anything when she tried to talk with intelligence. Granted, he didn't criticize her thinking: he just ignored it.

Solution.

Compliments can be dangerous even though they usually make us feel momentarily good. Nevertheless, one has to learn to take them in stride. If we can build a strong self-image, then compliments from others won't be so likely to sabotage our behavior. What matters most is what the individual thinks of himself and not what others value. If someone offers praise, it can be gracefully accepted without needing to justify it. It would be a most painful world if we all had to alter our behavior because someone else wanted it that way.

Manipulation By Parents

One would think that when two people marry they would be free from their parents. Unfortunately, such is often not the case. Let me again cite examples.

Mary had been married for over three years when she finally received the happy news from her doctor: she and her husband Joe were going to have a child. For two years they had hoped and prayed for this news. They were beginning to wonder if it would ever happen.

Mary rushed home to count the hours until Joe came home. She was bursting with joy when Joe finally arrived home. Joe suggested they go out to dinner to celebrate and later call their parents. For some reason that she couldn't understand, Mary was not anxious to call her mother.

When Joe insisted she did, she then understood her reluctance. Her mother was clearly not happy. Mary's mother had always wanted her daughter to have a career. She accepted her marriage to Joe and even seemed to like him. But she constantly told her daughter many married women still have careers. Her mother's reaction over the phone certainly dulled the dinner celebration.

The months flew by and finally the happy day arrived. Delivery was easy and the new parents were delighted with their young son, Joe Jr. Mary had done well from the beginning of her pregnancy right through delivery. She was happy about everything except her mother's attitude; she didn't seem pleased with becoming a grandmother.

To Mary's surprise and initial delight, her mother visited her soon after Mary brought Joey Jr. home from the hospital. Mary hoped that her mother would finally approve.

When she saw Joey, her mother did seem pleased. Later, however mother and daughter were immediately, locked in conflict. Everything Mary did was deemed wrong by her mother. She began to feel increasingly inadequate. Her mother brought out guilt feelings until Mary finally felt she might possibly be damaging to her son. Mary began to withdraw and allowed her mother to care for Joey.

The conflict then intensified. Mary gradually felt she was a bad housekeeper, bad wife, and bad mother.

She finally was so manipulated by her mother, she became dependent upon her and was consequently very depressed. For a time, Mary was literally manipulated right out of her home.

Sid and Nancy were also victims of intrusive inlaws. Since childhood, Sid's father never seemed to have confidence in his son. To hear his father Murray talk, Sid was incapable of even earning a living. Zelda, Sid's mother, wanted to tell Nancy how to treat Sid—how to handle the children and how to keep house. Sid allowed his parents to take over because he couldn't deal with his guilt. Everytime he tried to live his own life, his mother or father would say "Sidney, it's just that we love you and we want you to have the best in life." Their "best" for Sid almost resulted in his divorce.

Young couples must be free to make their own mistakes, to meet with success on their own, and to live their own lives. This does not mean that they cannot accept advice. All of us can profit from the wisdom of older, more experienced persons.

Giving advice and taking over by manipulative means are two very different things. No young couple can function well if they believe everything they do is wrong or inadequate. Therefore, one can welcome inlaws only so long as they abide by the rules, you establish. Limits sometimes need to be set. The couple can do much to help themselves if they stand united. You can thank Mom and Dad for their advice but indicate that, just as they had their ways, you both have yours. This is your home, this is your spouse, and these are your children. As much as you can, be free of hostility but be firm. The firmer you are, the less you will need to be angry.

Having Children

Tragically, many couples bring children into the world out of a sense of guilt. The wife feels that she must have a child because her husband wants her to. Or she may manipulate him because she wants to prove she is a woman. On the negative side, the wife may *deprive* her husband through guilt because she feels inadequate (and guilty) about becoming a mother. Sometimes she tricks him and gets pregnant, then manipulates him through guilt into staying in a marriage that he might otherwise have left.

Sometimes husbands need to prove that they are men or they want to live through a child. So, out of guilt, the wife consents. Some men can't be adequate parents and they know it. Feeling guilty, they agree to fatherhood and thus hold onto a woman that would otherwise have left them.

All of these instances are tragic because the child is the one most harmed. It takes maturity to rear children; guilt feelings will only cause hostility toward the child as well as the spouse. I would love to see marriages constituted to produce joy and growth for all concerned; one can only hope that someday we will see such a happy occurence. But, if parents are going to manipulate one another, let's learn to leave children out of it. They can be a great joy to us all—if we only give them half a chance!

Guilt And Divorce

Unfortunately, marriages frequently do not last until "death us do part." A look at the latest statistics show that around 40 percent of marriages fail. Alarmingly, too the figure seems on the rise.

There are many reasons why our divorce rate is so high. However, guilt reactions are often cited as a contributing factor. Many couples stay together almost solely out of guilt feelings. They are concerned about what will become of their children, what society may say; or the reaction of their parents.

In maintaining a marriage because of the children, however, one is likely to transmit guilt feelings to them. I often wonder whether that is the real reason, anyway. In my experience, when parents make that claim, they are very dependent people looking for an excuse to hold an immature relationship together. The children generally accept the reason given for staying together and carry an awful burden. I think there might be some question as to whether this helps or hurts them.

I am not one to advocate divorce but I do believe there are some circumstances when it is preferable to a life of misery. At least it does grant people a chance to gain freedom and then start over. If the pain outweighs the pleasure, one shouldn't allow guilt feelings to bind him to an unhappy marriage. I refer here to either his own guilt or the manipulation of a dependent partner.

There are some cases in which guilt feelings can actually cause a divorce. I think of one woman, Rose P. who I counselled for a time in therapy. She had been divorced once before and was beginning to work on her second divorce. Her husband Joe asked her to seek counseling as he did not want to dissolve the marriage.

I found Rose to be an extremely guilt-ridden woman who actually stillloved her husband. The problem was that she also felt worthless as a person; certainly insecurity had been a life-long problem. She had always felt great doubts about her adequacy as a woman. Thus, her push for a divorce was explained by her guilt at holding Joe to an "inadequate person." Her guilt feelings were compelling her to seek a divorce.

Happily, Rose was able to accept the interpretation that her insecurity and guilt were motivating her to do something that she really didn't want to do. She agreed to enter therapy and take a good look at herself. With her high level of motivation, she was able to solve her basic problems quickly. She found that as she felt more secure, she also felt more deserving of a good husband. Today this couple stands as an example of a happily married twosome.

Lois was another young woman who suffured from feelings of guilt. In her case, however, it was *because* she sought a divorce. Her husband Mike was, she said, a "very nice guy." Lois acknowledged that this fact made it doubly hard for her to seek a divorce. Mike had given Lois every imaginable freedom; he seemed not to have any very objectionable traits; and he was a good provider. He was shocked with her decision since he felt they were well suited to one another.

Lois would not talk about her reasons for the divorce but always insisted that she did not want a big alimony settlement. Then as the days passed, she seemed to be looking for some faults with Mike in order to justify her decision. She gradually succeeded in finding some, although mutual friends felt they were contrived. As she did so, her mood began to change: she became increasingly angry at Mike. She used terms such as "I could just kill him because of all those wasted years."

The emotional changes were accompanied by a new attitude towards the settlement. "Now I want every penny I can get. . .. I'll make him pay for everything he did to me," she often said. Indeed, there was some truth to her statement: the lawyer's fees alone amounted to a small fortune. Unfortunately, as a result of the long, drawn-out hearings, there was also less money for Lois.

Men, of course, are equally guilty. Sadly, the happy years become obscured by angry rhetoric. In addition, there is a terrible waste of money. If there are children, they often have sharply divided loyalties. Guilt reactions can do very destructive things to people. There are no easy answers in this struggle, because when people become emotional, they usually won't listen. It might not hurt, however to consider divorce counseling before making the break.

Divorce often has a shattering effect on all involved. Frequently the ones who did not initiate the divorce action become guilt-ridden and insecure. They feel that they are too inadequate to have any future relationships. They may become withdrawn and depressed.

The best thing to do is go right back into "circulation." I don't suggest jumping right into another marriage, but you should seek the company of others. Just because one relationship doesn't turn out, we can't conclude that none will. Divorced people are fortunate in several respects these days. With the high divorce rate, there are plenty of other available companions. Women can seek more agressive male companions; furthermore, there are more places to go to meet members of the opposite sex. Who knows? Maybe (as the song goes) it will be better the second time around? With a little more maturity and planning, it could be!

10

How Children Use Guilt to Manipulate

Children are masters at learning the rules of family interaction; the accuracy with which they describe their parents is amazing. In my practice, I often asked children about their parents; their responses led me to believe that children are more perceptive than adults. Perhaps this ability develops because parents are so significant and central in the child's world.

Anyone who understands another person well has a potential power over that person. The child must depend on his parents to satisfy most of his material needs. Therefore, it's in his interest to learn what behaviors and approaches will most often succeed in having those needs met. The child may become very adept at predicting the response of his parents.

Children do not deliberately set out to manipulate via guilt. Rather, they determine what works and use guilt only when it seems the most feasible approach. I believe that there are two important reasons why guilt works so well today. First of all, ours is a very child-oriented society and, consequently, there are many cultural norms that purport to tell us how "good" we are as parents. I don't believe in such norms; nevertheless, they do affect parents. For example, something a parent reads may suggest to him that he is a "bad" parent. Out of guilt he may wish to compensate to his child; he is then an easy target for manipulation.

Secondly, children and adolescents are more sophisticated today. They communicate much more with one another about the freedoms and privileges their parents grant them. Thus, they may claim their parents are not conforming to the behavior of their peers' parents; this can serve to justify demands on the part of the children.

This second point is exemplified by an experience I had talking to a group of parents. Repeatedly, they asked how they should set down norms of behavior for their children. I asked for particulars. One mother said that she did not want her son to stay out past 10P.M. o'clock on week nights. Her son told her that all his pals were allowed to stay out until 11:00 if they'd finished their homework. "All the kids can, Mom, and I'm the only one who has to be home so early."

His mother did not want to be overprotective, nor did she wish her son to be considered odd by his group. The town had no curfew, and when she saw her son's friends out late, she relented.

When she finished her story, another mother spoke up. Her son had tried the same approach; he had even cited the first mother's son as an example. Other parents spoke up and they soon realized that they had *all* been duped. The game worked as follows: Boy A says boy B gets to stay out late, and boy B says the same to his parents about boy A. Since the parents don't compare notes, the sons have manipulated their parents into believing that a fictitious norm of parental behavior exists.

Later I heard a similar story regarding mini-bikes. The Jones boy got his parents to agree that he could have a mini-bike if the Smith boy got one. The Smith boy worked the same angle; then both simultaneously reported to their parents that the other boy was getting a mini-bike. Since the parents didn't call each other, both boys got their bikes.

After the stories of manipulation were revealed, the initial parental reaction was one of laughter; then they became very angry. I anticipated that many were eager to punish their children, but that didn't seem to be the best answer. When the anger dissipated, I told the parents that they had set themselves up for this trouble: had they not been so easily manipulated all of this would not have happened.

I suggested an alternate approach: You should be

able to justify any rules you set. You can always examine and discuss the validity of these reasons. When there is a question of what is appropriate, get further information directly from someone else. But don't crumble to the demands of conformity. After all, conformity should not be the basis for principles of discipline: the fact that "everyone is doing it" does not make "it" right.

Today children acquire a great deal of information from television, and that too may be used to manipulate parents. Just imagine the variety of toys that are shown on television in a given year. Children can always point to something that they don't have. Thus, television provides a ready appraisal of whether you are keeping up with the Jones.

Stores are also common scenarios of attempted manipulation. As soon as a child walks in with you he sees a dozen things he needs. Sometimes you'll hear the phrase, "Can I buy just *one*?" Of course the implication here is that if you refuse such a modest purchase you are pretty stingy. What parent can face that accusation?

Teenage girls are adept at manipulating their parents for new clothing. If mom won't bend, maybe dad will; thus a girl can attempt to play her parents against each other. Some typical approaches are: "I haven't got anything to wear," "I have a closet full of clothes but I want something new." Or there is the "Mary Jones just got a new dress for the party and *she* will steal the show."

I believe it's very dangerous to yield to this sort of manipulation. If you are manipulated into making unnecessary purchases for your children, sooner or later you will punish them with your anger. Indulging them certainly doesn't encourage an appreciation of the value of a dollar. They need parental guidance for that; without adequate supervision, they will never learn how to set responsible guidelines for their behavior.

Parents need to set realistic limits. Without parental leadership, the child will never learn to set guidelines for himself.

I suggest two approaches. First, establish a reasonable allowance for your child or adolescent. Then teach him the value of money by allowing him to make most of his own purchases. Let him make his own mistakes. He may want to spend all of his money on a toy car—only to regret it later. Allow him to do this but don't give in when he does. Point out that we all make mistakes but that he has learned a valuable lesson.

A second approach is to involve him in the family financial decision-making process. If you are considering a purchase, let him know the extent of what you are willing to spend. Give him choices so that he is involved in deciding which item to buy. You'll find that children can handle reality very well.

Through the years I have found that many parents have questions about disciplining their children. I know from experience that differing viewpoints on discipline can provoke marital conflict. Most parents sense that their methods of disciplining children leave something to be desired and want to do better.

I don't believe that a disciplinary program need be all that complicated; of course, problems start as soon as guilt feelings enter the picture. Most children know how to provoke guilt feelings in their parents after they have been disciplined. So the parents see-saw back and forth, from overly strict to overly lax approaches. Punishment is meted out; guilt sets in; limits become too lax; anger sets in, and the cycle is completed with excessive discipline.

The solution is not very complicated, even though it may be hard to put into effect. Remember to discipline on principle, not anger. Set limits before you become angry, and punish out of procedure and not anger. When you become angry, two things happen: children become fearful and don't learn, and they become angry and don't want to please. When you do set your goals or rules, above all, be consistent. Children will at first try to get you to relax the constraints. When they find the rules are fixed, they will follow them.

I caution against name calling, which is extremely destructive. Never call a child "bad" or "stupid." It is his behavior you wish to correct; you don't want to smash his self-concept. Allow him to discuss his feelings but don't change your goals unless reason dictates. I firmly believe you can avoid harsh physical punishment if you consistently discipline before you are angry. Children learn by example; if you constantly threaten but don't follow through, your child will be confused.

Let us finally consider the child who induces guilt by underachievement in school. They are telling you as a parent that you have failed them. Avoid being overprotective. Try to get the youngster to take responsibility for his own behavior. Set limits that will help him build self-discipline.

Some children learn to use illness to escape disciplinary actions. Be careful you don't bend to manipulation and change rules arbitrarily. Recognize the extent of the illness and proceed from there.

For example, little Johnny says he has a headache; out of guilt you allow him to miss school. You may feel badly because you tried to force him to attend school. An hour later he is running around the house with no evidence of that head-splitter. Remember, if he is too ill for school, he is certainly too ill to run around. Tell him that he can stay in his room or go to the doctor. Stick to those choices and his ploy will no longer work.

In summary, remember that your child can't manipulate you unless you give him permission. Prevent manipulation with consistent and fair guidelines for behavior. Base your code on what is really good for both you and your child; in that way, there is no need for anyone to feel guilty.

11

Parents, Guilt and Manipulation

In handling children, the use of guilt is an accepted and often unchallenged practice. Many parents openly admit to the deliberate use of guilt; they claim that it is the only alternative to the threat of physical violence that will successfully control a child's behavior. On an unconscious level, guilt is used more widely than is commonly recognized. Since children have little recourse in this situation, much abuse goes unnoticed.

In this chapter, I would like to call attention to the misuse of guilt in disciplinary problems, citing other, more effective techniques for changing behavior. Given alternatives, we can prevent the crippling development of severe guilt reactions which characteristically begin early in life.

Very early in life children are labelled by their parents as good or bad: "He was a very good baby."

Let's consider what the parent is really saying. Like teachers who praise the docile child for being "good," the parent is commending the child who doesn't make waves and is quiet and nondemanding. A "good" baby is one who sleeps through the night, does not frequently wet and doesn't have eating problems.

Secondly, what are we saying to the older child who wasn't a "good baby?" By labelling him, we are setting up negative expectations for him to live up (or down) to. Effective change becomes that much harder. Often the child becomes resigned to his "bad" reputation and feels no desire to please. In his mind, it is too late anyway.

He may also go in the opposite direction. Excessively dependent, he is afraid to venture far from his parents because he is constantly hoping to win their approval. He only displeases the parent further: few people consciously want their children to be withdrawn, rebellious or excessively dependent.

Perceptive parents recognize the effect their attitudes have on children's behavior. For example, some particularly insightful parents have told me they were uncomfortable from the beginning with the child who turned out to be the bad baby. Frequently, the first baby is labelled "difficult" because the parents feel especially insecure. Other factors that figure in determining attitudes are: having the child, marital conflict and financial strain.

The mother's role is especially important since she is the one who is closest to the child. She is also the one who must go through childbirth; if she has a difficult time in labor, she may feel strong hostility toward the child afterwards.

Infants are very sensitive to the emotional attitudes of those around them. Some may not sleep well because they sense parental tensions. Many eating difficulties also result from this.

As adults, we experience this phenomenon daily. We all hate to be around a particular person because they seem cold or angry. Consider how much worse it is for the infant who is dependent upon parents for his very existence.

Parents who deny their negative feelings towards their children do so out of guilt. They do not dare express what they feel. So they simply blame the child. In the process, they make the child responsible for their own guilt. That lays the basis for the guilt-ridden child.

Solving this problem isn't easy. Certainly, making mothers more comfortable, less fearful and more secure throughout pregnancy and delivery will help somewhat. Ventilating feelings helps, too. Looking at our negative feelings makes us better able to control and handle them. I also believe that planning for the birth of the child is constructive. The wanted child, coming when a family is ready for him, comes into a happier home.

As children grow older, they encounter other kinds of guilt-producing situations. Marital conflict is one such situation. Just imagine what happens to the boy who reminds his mother of his father. Or the girl who the father sees as being like his wife. There may also be crossed sex-identification which is the hatred of some trait that is like one parent possesses.

Many parents have told me that they become angry at their children when there is marital conflict. Mother punishes the son because he reminds her of her husband, this in turn, produces guilt. The reverse is true of fathers. In cases like this, the child is manipulated simply because he imitates the people who are around him. Actually, there is no one else with whom to identify.

Sometimes the child is punished because he possesses one of the parent's unacceptable traits. For example, a mother once told me that her son made her very angry. "He is so much like I am—timid, dependent and passive." That may have been true, but her anger will only reinforce these traits in the child's personality.

There is another variety of parent-child interaction that clearly produces a very destructive guilt reaction. This generally takes place after a disciplinary action or when the child is not allowed to do something he wants. The child doesn't say anything but clearly looks angry. Seeing the anger, the parent, in turn, becomes angry and threatens the child with additional punishment. When that happens, the child begins to feel guilty: not only for his actions but, also for his feelings.

I can well recall a youngster like this: I saw Johnny in play therapy for nearly a year and a half. His mother brought him to our clinic on his teacher's recommendation. Johnny was a beautiful little boy who had a charming smile (when it was permitted to show). On the few occasions where I heard him laugh, it reminded me of a bubbling brook.

Johnny was a physically active 10-year-old, but he seemed emotionally withdrawn. He was quiet in his classroom and seemed to become sullen whenever there was talk about aggressiveness.

One day, walking into the playroom, I accidently

stepped on Johnny's foot. I knew it hurt but he did not react with either pain or anger. Instead he said over and over, "That's okay, Dr Gunn." He was telling me that I need not worry; he wasn't angry. I carefully explained to Johnny that, when we are hurt, we automatically become angry. Humans don't like pain. "I feel angry at times, too, Johnny but I don't have to hit people."

All Johnny could do was deny his feelings. It took many weeks before I gained his confidence to the point where he would talk about his feelings. When he did open up, I had to make many promises that I wouldn't tell his mother. As Johnny talked, it became very clear that he was more guilt-ridden about his angry feelings than about his behavior. He felt that he could control his behavior but not his feelings.

While I worked with Johnny, a co-worker saw his mother. Gradually the story emerged. Johnny's mother was herself a guilt-ridden, anxious woman. She was afraid of losing control and she was especially afraid, therefore, of her anger.

When she punished Johnny, she could see his feeling of anger. In those days, Johnny was a very expressive boy. The sight of anger caused her alarm: she could not tolerate in others that which she could not accept in herself. Seeing Johnny's anger, she would announce that she knew he was angry, and "If you show me anger like that, son, you will really get it." So Johnny associated his angry feelings with more threats of severe punishment. The only way to avoid punishment was to hide all feelings. Angry feelings produced guilt because it made mother angry.

Johnny's improvement coincided with changes in his mother. As she learned to accept her own feelings, she no longer had to make Johnny guilty for his. She let him feel angry and even helped him find suitable outlets for his anger. Discipline was still firm but Johnny had the right to talk about how he felt. Johnny soon became a guilt-free, buoyant and happy child again.

Just as Johnny's mother felt guilty when she punished him, so do many other parents. Their guilt produces two very bad results. One is an inconsistency of rules. It goes like this: a rule is made, parents feel guilty, they don't enforce the rule, and the child becomes confused by the inconsistency. He isn't sure what his parents really want.

Secondly, the guilt causes the parents to try to justify their actions. They must then work to convince their child that his behavior was especially awful. Overkill causes the child to feel that he must *really* be very bad. The end result, as with inconsistency of rules, is apt to be rebellion. When anyone feels they have hit rock bottom, they lose interest in satisifying others. So they don't try at all.

The idea of fear and guilt about one's feelings reminds me of another child I saw years ago. Cindy R. came to our clinic with complaints of very bad nightmares. She often woke up screaming, realizing that something was wrong, her parents sought help. They had no idea what might be causing her fears.

Cindy proved to be a very open child and it was easy to establish rapport with her. With very little prompting, she began to talk about her guilt feelings. Cindy was actually the one who opened up the very pertinent discussion.

"Is it true," she wanted to know, "that when you wish something on someone else, it happens to you?" "Well, let's see, Cindy: if I wish that you got a thousand pounds of ice cream, would I get all that ice cream?"

Cindy laughed, "No, I mean something bad." I asked where she got that idea, and gradually the whole story came out. A year before when Cindy was barely 8-years-old she became angry at one of her teachers. Her teacher had not liked one of her projects and sent a note home. Cindy's mother had forced her to miss a television show that night, insisting she re-do the project. Angrily Cindy said, "Oh darn, she sees every mistake I make. I wish she would go blind."

Cindy's mother became fearful of the "hate wish," and punished Cindy. She told her that the things we wish for others happen to us. Cindy didn't say much at the time but on the inside, she was scared stiff. Feeling guilty for what she said she begged forgiveness "so it wouldn't happen to her." Cindy's guilt caused her to live in fear over what might happen in the future. It went further than that, however. Every time she had a "bad thought" about someone else, she worried that it would happen to her. The more compulsively she tried to avoid "bad thoughts," the more they came to mind.

Generally, the fostering of guilt feelings in children is an unconscious process. Parents seldom sit down and rationally decide to use this kind of manipulation to stop their children from saying "bad things." My experience dictates that such parents suffer great pangs of guilt and anxiety themselves when their children make those wishes. The parents seem to unconsciously believe their children will evoke destruction on them too, because they are somehow responsible for their children.

Fear and guilt, therefore, become transferred from one generation to the next. The child perceives both the parent's fear and anxiety. I believe that it is insufficient to treat the guilt of the child alone. Something needs to be done to help the parents as well. Usually this situation requires a kind of therapeutic discussion in which the parent re-examines his own fear and guilt. When most parents lose their fears, they cease manipulating their children.

Children can very easily be made to feel guilty about an illness. I recall Mr. Johnson, a very nervous salesman I saw years ago. He knew that he felt irritable when his sales record slumped. Perhaps because of his inner tension, he required much more sleep than average.

Unfortunately, Mr. Johnson's son, Mark, was prone to a number of minor illnesses. He had frequent colds, tended to run a fever easily, and had a number of allergies. One can well understand why an 11-year-old with breathing difficulties would find it difficult to sleep.

Of course, this meant that when Mark was unable to sleep, so was his father. Mr. Johnson would stomp into Mark's bedroom and remind him that he needed his sleep to work the next day. Often he would blame Mark for being sick. Any 10 year old will occasionally do foolish things like getting his feet wet or going out without a coat on cool days. Mark's careless actions gave his father ammunition. As a result Mark's illnesses then caused him to become guilt-ridden and overly cautious.

Mark was caught in a double-bind. After a sleepless night, Mr. Johnson would feel somewhat ill. Then he would accuse Mark of making him ill. As a result, Mark had to bear the brunt of guilt for: his father's poor sales record and his father's illness. With such a heavy burden of guilt, Mark was afraid to do anything. He would frequently refuse to go out and play like the other youngsters did. He gradually became more dependent upon his parents.

As that happened, Mark soon found out his father was still not pleased with him. Mark's increasing dependency placed heavy demands upon his parents, which precipitated marital conflicts. That, in turn made Mr. Johnson even more nervous: his problems at work increased correspondingly.

Obviously, Mr. Johnson's tenseness was a personal problem that warranted attention. He needed to learn to relax more and to stop blaming others for his problems. His use of guilt even made him ineffectual as a disciplinarian. Fortunately, he entered psychotherapy and became a happier, more relaxed person. As a result, he was free to achieve more success at work and at home.

Since children readily respond to the feelings of their parents, they can pick up fears as a result of their close identification. One problem in handling parental fears is that adults are loathe to admit we fear anything. This is generally more true of men than women. It is just not considered masculine to have a bunch of little phobias.

Unfortunately, though, when parents are not aware of what they feel, they can't help their children avoid the same phobias. In fact, parental denial produces a guilt conflict within the child. Children then are made to feel that their parents are liars. They are always concerned that their parents will see that they don't agree with what the parent reports. I have seen any number of parents claim they have no fears whatsoever. When I glance at the child, his face turns red, and he tries unconvincingly to support the parent's claim. Children consequently become guilt prone because they fear they will let their parents down.

Some parents recognize their fears but refuse to discuss them. The loathing of the fear exists but the parent never comes to grips with it. I have seen many instances when the child picks up the parental fear and is then ridiculed for it. Since the parents hate their fear, they punish it when it shows up in their child. There are apparently two factors in this behavior. The parents feel shame because the family secret is out. The hope that they might rear a fearless child (and in so doing master their own fears) is frustrated. This is a type of role reversal where, in a sense, the child becomes the parent. It seldom works. In the process, the child feels guilty for letting his parents down.

I would unequivocally suggest that a parent never shame a child for having phobic reactions. It will only make the situation worse. Instead, try to understand the fear and help the child do the same. Another helpful step would be for the parent to admit his own fears and try to deal with them. He might even give the child permission to reverse his phobias. This can only be done through open discussion-never by use of guilt.

There is another way that manipulation by guilt defeats parental goals. That involves attempts to teach children to be thrifty and save money. I can best illustrate what can go wrong by the example of ten-year-old Bobby S. Bobby's parents were very money-conscious—so much so that for a time I wondered whether my bill would be paid.

It was very important to Bobby's parents that he learn to save his money. Given an allowance from the time he was 8-years-old, he was also paid for odd jobs that he did around the house. He was told to keep his money in a bank until he had saved 15 dollars. At that point, it was to be transferred to a savings account.

Bobby was initially eager about earning and saving money. The only problem was that he also wanted to spend some of his money. That was where the problem first developed. When he asked to buy something with his money, his parents convinced him that his purchase would be foolish. Bobby did not argue, but he finally began robbing his own piggy bank. When that happened, his parents treated him as if he was dishonest.

Gradually, Bobby became very guilt-ridden about money. Because of his guilt, he stopped trying to spend it. The trouble was he also lost interest in money: it was no longer a valuable commodity. He stopped doing those little extra jobs and did not even seem to care about his allowance. His parents wondered why.

Actually, the reason is very simple. His parents robbed Bobby of the opportunity to learn how to handle money. If you never spend any money, you can't learn how to use it wisely. You can't profit by foolish purchase and there is never any joy in saving for something you want. Conceptually, the bank is far away to a child; the future seems even more remote. Savings "interest" is basically an abstract term that children do not understand. To Bobby, his money no longer existed; it was earned by him, but he felt it was actually owned and controlled by his parents. He would have learned more if he could have spent it.

I firmly believe that many parents go too far in protecting a child from failure. Overprotection stops growth and causes dependency. For example, if a parent does a great deal for a child and then constantly reminds him of it, there is bound to be a guilt reaction. I have sometimes sat in on a family interview when the parents couldn't stop talking about all they did for a child. I have wanted to say "All right, all ready—that's enough." By the time the parent finishes, you wonder how the child can dare to open his mouth.

Of course, the answer is to avoid overdoing it. Children have to learn to face reality. When they enter the real world (as when they go to school), no one is going to do everything for them. When you give something to a child, give it willingly. Don't remind him of it all the time.

I believe that, in general, parents make the mistake of overprotecting daughters more than sons. Mothers spend a great deal of time in selecting their daughters' clothes and grooming her. Neither father nor mother set many limits on the amount of money spent on her clothing. Fathers are probably the softer touch: a father will more likely refuse a son's requests than a daughter's. When a girl becomes interested in sports, she is often told that she isn't expected to try very hard. She doesn't have to be strong: her parents seem to not want her to be tough-minded.

How does all of this affect the girl? Well, as we will probably all agree, the girl finds it more difficult to be assertive. She can't easily stand up for her rights. She is inclined to feel guilt if she does something better than a boy. I can still recall two young girls that I saw professionally who felt very guilty because they had beaten all the boys in their class at swimming. Other girls have felt guilty because they were the best students in their class. This type of guilt reaction robs one of personal identity.

There is also another factor influencing the situation. With everything done for the girl, it becomes more difficult for her to stand on her own two feet. She may want to leave home in her late teen years but can't. She is unable to consider a career. The girl often becomes so dependent on her parents that she can't imagine a life apart from theirs: marriage and a family. Many girls work only out of necessity or at the expense of guilt reactions.

Early in the child's life, parents often start outlining the directions and goals to be achieved. For the girl, there are all kinds of directives on the type of man she must marry.

"I only want my little girl to be happy," many parents proclaim. How can a daughter object to that? Many can't and so they become manipulated by their guilt feelings. Every man they like is deemed "not good enough." When the girl gets into her early twenties, the push is on. She must get married: mom and dad want a grandchild. Caution goes out the window and many girls are manipulated into unhappy marriages.

The boy, on the other hand, encounters a different type of manipulation. Dad only wants him to enjoy sports. So dad spends long hours teaching him to throw and catch a ball. His son responds and seems to enjoy sports. How could he do otherwise after all of dad's sacrifices? The trouble is Dad is never satisified with his performance. So there is more manipulation through guilt and never much fun or relaxation.

Many parents live their lives through their children in this manner. One young man told me that he had graduated third in his high school class and only a point from first. He rushed home to tell his father, glowing with pride. His father only remark was: "Oh fine, son, who was first?" The son said he was devastated. He felt guilt-ridden because he sensed he let his father down.

The answer to these problems is to allow your children to do their own thing. Help them set priorities but don't try to live their lives for them. Support them when they feel they have done something well. This helps children strive for higher levels. Pushing, on the other hand, eventually causes people to tire and give up.

Finally, there are two ways of manipulating children that I have frequently seen in my clinical practice. Generally I have come to believe that these abuses are correctable only through professional help. This is indicated because: they usually involve unconscious behavior on the part of the parent, and are deeply ingrained personality traits.

The first involves the overprotective, dependent parent. Their entire lives are centered around their children and they don't allow their children to separate from them. They use an approach like: "Life at home answers all of your needs. Why would you want to leave?"

In fact, the dependent ones are the parents. They can't stand to be without their children, and live through them; as the children mature, they reverse roles. They blame their children if they are unhappy: some of these parents go overboard in discussing their personal problems with their children. The child gradually begins to feel guilty whenever he thinks of spending time away from home. Some children even become so dependent that they can't separate from their parents.

The second kind of manipulation involves what we might call expectations. In "positive expectation " situations, the parents overload the child with praise. Some typical comments are: "He is perfect; he would never do that, he can always be trusted," or "You know, dear, I never have to worry about you." It is one thing to have trust: it is another to set impossible, rigid standards. With such parental "trust," how can the child ever do anything even a little naughty. If he does, he will surely suffer. Usually, children who have this kind of parent are rigid, emotionally flat, unadventuresome and ultra-conservative.

There is also another sort of message regarding expectations technically termed the "double bind." Professionals also refer to the parents's expectations as involving "mixed messages." This type of manipulation is complicated and very destructive to children.

It goes something like this. A parent states that he just wants his children to obey or to be socially acceptable or successful. Thus, on the surface, the stated message is, "I want you to perform well." Unfortunately, though, this message is inaccurate. The parent doesn't really expect anything to go well. Such people are terribly guilt-ridden and fear they possess severe failings as parents.

Their deeper expectations are that their children will get into some kind of trouble. I have seen over a hundred such cases. They range from the mother who *just knew* her daughter would get pregnant to the father who always expected his son to steal.

A case in point was the teenage boy I saw two weeks ago. He had run away from home twice in the past year. When I met the mother and son for the first time, she immediately announced that she hoped I didn't have a back door to my office. "I am afraid my son will run off, Dr. Gunn," she announced. Had she truly been concerned, she should have mentioned that on the phone when she made the appointment.

Negative expectations such as this are a warning to the child. If he fails to carry out the expectation, his parent is wrong. In that case, his parents feel guilty because they seem to be expecting the worst without reason. Many times I am challenged when I attempt to explain this to the parent.

Okay, Dr. Gunn, I won't expect the worst but you will see: he will do it anyway!"

Under those circumstances I know that he will; the underlying message has not changed. If you practice this type of manipulation with your children, try to take a good look at what you are doing as a parent. I realize that it is difficult to examine ourselves, but in seeking help, we may save a child's future.

Not all problems between children and parents can be easily solved. Manipulation is sneaky and often hard to detect. But try giving praise when it is well earned; have faith; set solid, consistent limits; and try to open the lines of communication. You may just discover the true joy of being a parent.

12

Guilt at Work in Our Schools

Quite a few years of my professional practice have been connected in some manner with schools, both as a teacher and a test administrator in schools. I've also done clinical consultation with teachers and have run teacher improvement programs. In all that time, I have never failed to be struck by the widespread use of manipulation by guilt that exists in our school program. I sometimes wonder if any other techniques have had such wide application.

Guilt, I believe, is very widely used for several reasons: the false belief that children must be coerced into learning, and the lack of imagintion and rigidity of so many teachers. These two factors and perhaps others have caused formal education to be a massive manipulator.

First, something needs to be said about our concept of learning. I often wonder whether most of the adult world doesn't still feel guilty about our own school days. When I talk with most adults, I find that they remember disliking school—for certain social activities that took place in high school or college. The academic part seldom seems to have been pleasant. In particular, most people recall that they disliked grade school.

Unfortunately, many parents have rationalized their own dislike for school instead of trying to change the system. "It is necessary," they say, "and no children can like that which is mandatory. Therefore, we must torture our children because otherwise they will be unprepared for life. Learning can't be fun."

I disagree most heartily with this concept. I will readily agree that not all learning is fun, but then, not all of *any* activity is fun. I love to play golf, but it isn't fun to get sand in one's eye when exploding out of a sand trap. I accept this, but because golf is vastly more pleasurable than painful, I do play whenever I can.

The same applies to school: children need merely to have some fun. If they do, they will accept the unpleasant. All healthy children have a desire to learn. They are inquisitive, and they ask questions by the thousands; they search everywhere for new experiences. Some parents complain to me that they wish the quest for learning were not so great: little Johnny gets into everything.

What, then, turns our children off to the learning experience? I am definitely not going to blame the schools entirely. With plenty of outside help, the school does bear a large responsibility, however, I actually believe our school system often stops rather than enhances the child's desire to learn.

I have one illustration of this that is so vivid and easily understood that I want to present it at once.

Children are very much like adults even though we often forget this. Now, let us suppose that you, the reader, told me you enjoyed dancing. We might then assume that you would go dancing whenever the opportunity arose.

What would happen, however, if I were to put you on some entertainment committee that required you to dance five hours a night, five nights a week? (You might reach the point where you would dislike dancing.) Let's make it more applicable to the child's situation. Let us suppose again that I somehow forced you to dance when you didn't do your job. I made you feel guilty and, as such, you accepted your punishment. I will bet you would now grow to hate dancing.

On to the child's world. Little Johnny was "bad;" he accepts this verdict. He now needs to feel guilty and to be punished. His punishment will be to write, 25 times, "I won't disobey my teacher." As he writes, he feels resentment and guilt at being forced to do something. Writing then becomes something associated with guilt, punishment, force, and embarrassment. Does that make writing fun? Is that situation any different from the adult who had to dance?

Some will claim it *is,* saying children don't like to write in the first place. I disagree. Children see magic when a marker of some sort hits the paper. When they learn to write their names, they often plant their names everywhere. They draw, color, scribble and write because it is, for them, a new, enchanting exercise in power and self-definition.

My own children have sent me copious notes asking questions, making statements and playing games. But when writing becomes guilt-ridden punishment, that destroys the fun. I can still recall the occasion when Buddy came home after having to write, "I will not run in the halls," 25 times. His comment, "I'm beginning to learn to hate writing," sums it up well. Notice that he said "learn to hate,"which is exactly what the process is. It seems to me any teacher that has to resort to this type of discipline is awfully rigid and lacking in imagination. Such rigidity never allows one to work well with children.

My own teaching experience provided me with some insights into what takes place in the minds of some teachers. I was teaching at the time in a junior college and had several beginning classes in psychology. It had been a general rule of the college that attendance had to be rigidly enforced. I felt then as now that people of college age should take responsibility for preparing themselves for exams. If they miss class, they will likely have more trouble with their exams. If they do not have such trouble then they ought not to be penalized.

At several meetings of faculty members, attendance was always discussed. Most of the teachers felt students should be penalized through lowered grades if they missed over four classes per semester. The administration was very flexible, however, and left the policy on grading to the individual teacher. Attendance records were required because of state funding.

At the end of my second year, I met four other teachers who were complaining about their low attendance. They said that, despite penalities, their students frequently missed class.

"I have tried everything I know to make these kids feel guilty about wasting their money, their time and my time, but they still cut classes," a teacher said.

Several asked me questions about my classes, and one teacher said that he had heard I had the best attendance record at the college. He said he was surprised because it was reported that I didn't penalize students for absences.

"That's right, I don't, but the students seem to want to come to class," I answered.

Someone else then said, "Oh sure, Dr. Gunn is lucky. Psychology is interesting but it's hard to get kids to come to something as dry as history." Each of the others made the same comment about their classes. I felt that here was the answer: the teachers *themselves* found the subject matter boring. They actually felt guilty about subjecting the students to such course content. If someone feels guilty, he will punish others for his guilt feelings: that is just what they were doing. But, in addition, how can you teach something you do not like? A teacher is very much like a salesman: he is selling an interest in history or government or psychology. You can't sell a product if you do not believe in it yourself.

I wondered then why these people were teaching. When I asked some of the teachers this question, I received some very disappointing answers. "What else could you do with a major in anthropology?" Or "I tried business but I found I wasn't suited for it.". Or "I'm going to school myself but until I finish school I need to have some job."

That was most discouraging to me. These people have the future of our next generation in their hands. They are supposed to inspire people: to help keep alive the joy of learning. Often, the only reason a youngster originally likes a particular area of learning is because he liked the teacher. If a teacher feels ambivalent about his "boring" subject, the student will also feel guilt when he studies that subject. He is likely to lose interest.

I saw another example of guilt in our school system when I was hired to do some intelligence testing in a full school district. This meant testing all of the children in, say the fourth grade at nine different schools. The teachers had been told ahead of time to prepare an alphabetized list of all of the students in their respective classes.

I was absolutely amazed when I saw the lists. Some were done perfectly with clear, easy-to-read writing. Still other lists were badly out-of-order (the writing was nearly illegible), with simple names such as David or Charles misspelled. I thought perhaps the misspellings were careless mistakes until I saw severely misspelled words written on the chalkboards. The grammar of some of the teachers was terrible, in contrast to others who spoke very well. I happened to hear one teacher tell a pupil, "You gots no business hanging around outside: you should have went into the school when the bell was runged."

When I later talked to the superintendent of the school, the quality of the teachers arose. He was Caucasian, but said he was proud that he always tried to hire black or other minority teacher applicants where possible.

"Well, that's fine," I said, "But it seems to me that teachers should be selected only if they are well qualified."

He became angry and I received a long lecture on how difficult it was for a black teacher to be hired somewhere. I surely wasn't against the poor, the black, and other minorities, was I?

"No, indeed I am not," I replied, still not feeling guilty about my observation. "But it looks to me as if most of the less qualified minority teachers end up in the nearly all black schools."

"Well, of course, they do, Dr. Gunn," he shot back. "The parents from the 'white sections' demand the best; they pay a lot to support our school district."

Granted, but that meant many of the students who especially needed skilled teachers instead got the very worst. I later suggested to the school board that it was fine to look for a percentage of black or Latino teachers but I was sure they could find well qualified ones. They might even offer in-service training programs to help prepare the less skilled teachers. I was delighted that the black members of the school board did not think of my remarks as "racist." They didn't try to make me feel guilty and put into effect some of my recommendations. I guess they were interested primarily in the children!

It seems to me there is a tremendous push for conformity in our school system. In order to achieve this conformity, manipulation by guilt is widely used. I witnessed this as a child, and I still see it as an adult.

I still remember a very painful situation that happened as a child. My grade school days coincided in part with WW II. Of course, it was patriotic to buy as many war bonds and stamps as one could afford. In our school, the teachers set up a reward system for those classes that bought the greatest amount of war bonds and had the highest percentage of students buying at least one war stamp. There were special awards to both the winning classroom and the teacher of that classroom.

Our room always did well as far as the overall total was concerned but we never hit the 100 percent participation level. There were two students who never purchased stamps or bonds: the plain fact was that they couldn't afford them. From their clothes, it appeared they barely had sufficient funds for apparel.

Our teacher exalted us every week to do what we could for the war effort. "Your stamp might save a boy's life," was a rather familar phrase. Then the push began for total participation; at the end of collection each Friday, the teacher would announce how we had done. We did basically the same each week: 34 out of 36.

The pressure began to pile up on the two pupils who never made any purchases. The teacher would make an announcement something like this on Wednesdays: "Okay, we have done well this week, class, but let's see if this Friday we can't get everyone to buy at least one stamp. You know, I feel pretty sure that we can all afford at least a quarter for our fighting men."

Sometimes other pupils would turn around and stare

at the two nonbuyers. With increasing frequency I noticed these two students were absent on Friday. That seemed to please the teacher because she then got her perfect record.

Not surprisingly, we began to have some petty thefts around the school. The thefts never involved more than a quarter. Coincidentally, a few days later, the two kids who had not purchased stamps did so for the first time. Now they were really in trouble: when the teacher issued warnings on stealing, these two really suffered. One began to develop what is now called a school phobia and he seemed to be afraid to come to school.

A friend of mine, he swore he never stole any money around school. He told me he felt very guilt-ridden because he had taken the money from his mother's purse. I believed him but he could not admit his crime around school. Since he felt so much personal guilt, he always looked guilty when subtly accused by the teacher. I know that school became unbearable for him.

I think the idea of motivating school children through guilt is a dreadful crime. Several years ago, I saw a girl who had developed a very severe learning disorder. Janet was a bright girl who had always done well in school. She had seemed to enjoy school and relished time spent there. Her mother told me she seemed basically happy but was a bit on the serious side.

Her mood began to change rather sharply in the fourth grade. It seemed Janet was never a very strong speller although she had never been noticeably poor, either. The fourth-grade teacher felt that the children could be motivated to become better at spelling if they had a weekly competition. The team approach was used to let the youngsters know that if they did poorly they let down "not only yourselves but your whole team." There were special rewards for the winning team that ranged from money to extra recess. The prizes were of sufficient significance to the children that winning became very important.

In the first contest, it was Janet who made the difference. She missed three of the four words given and caused her team to lose. As I recall, her team lost by only one word; had Janet improved her performance by one answer, there would have been a tie. In the event of a tie, the best speller, or "captain," of each team was involved in a kind of play-off. The captain of Janet's team was vastly better than anyone else, so a tie was tantamount to victory.

Janet's teammates were understandably unhappy with her performance and told her so. The teacher intervened, saying that what was done was done, but she was sure Janet would improve the following week. Of course, she was adding to Janet's already considerable amount of guilt. It is one thing to let down your teammates, but it is worse to let down a teacher who has professed faith in you.

As one might expect, the following week went the same as the first. Janet failed, despite the fact that she had worked hard all week. She apparently became so tense she missed two words that she had practiced at home all week. Her teammates were again very irritated with her and Janet sought to defend herself by saying perhaps she just wasn't good at spelling. Unfortunately, the teacher took that defense away from her by telling everyone she knew Janet could do well if she tried harder. In front of other students the teacher told Janet that girls generally are better spellers than boys; what was wrong with her?

Now the pressure intensified with the implication that perhaps Janet wasn't trying as hard as she might. Though a few of the more friendly girls tried to help her, Janet wanted to go it on her own. She naturally did not wish to flaunt her ignorance, but the other girls inferred that to mean Janet didn't want their help.

Janet was luckier the following week: she wasn't at school. She developed a mysterious headache and her mother kept her home. Without her presence, her team won; there were quite a few malicious remarks acknowledging her absence. The teacher defended her, but that was like a kiss of death. The other students felt that Janet was a teacher's pet and they began to openly ridicule her.

The fourth week's competition was a repeat of the humiliation Janet received during the first two contests. Once again Janet had not felt well but her mother did not allow her to miss school. She had asked Janet if there were something wrong but her daughter was too ashamed to tell the story to her mother. When Janet began to do poorly in the fourth round, some of her teammates began to joke about a trade. "Why not? Baseball teams trade players," some of the more brazen joked.

When Janet's team lost for the third time in four contests, the teacher decided that perhaps new teams should be selected each week. When that system was put into effect, Janet was subjected to a new kind of ridicule. The captains would not only select her last but they attempted to overlook her. This treatment only pointed up her inadequacies.

The situation worsened when the teacher decided to pick Janet for a team captain one week. That way, her teacher reasoned, Janet would not always be selected last. As nearly everyone would guess, those picked by Janet begged off. "Don't pick me, Janet," was a frequently heard phrase.

As the situation progressed, Janet grew to dislike school more and more. Consequently, her grades began to drop in her other classes. Her mother saw mood changes and noted her daughter's ever-increasing reluctance to even attend school. She began to suspect her daughter was developing emotional problems and it was at that point that she brought her daughter to me.

Fortunately, Janet had not lost her ability to communicate, and I was quickly able to locate the problem. Janet had a good rapport with her parents and so we had some strengths to build on. Later I visited the school and talked to Janet's teacher.

I felt sure her teacher felt some guilt feelings over what had taken place. But, as so often happens, the guilt-ridden seek to manipulate others. If the blame could be shifted to Janet, then the teacher's guilt would subside. It is always easy to blame children because they don't have the reasoning power or the psychological defenses to fight back. Janet's teacher tried to criticize Janet and both her parents in order to shift the blame.

I decided to work around the guilt and told the

teacher it didn't really matter who was to blame. We now had a bad situation on our hands; for Janet's sake we had to make some changes. "I will work with her parents. Will you give me some help at school?" I asked.

"Of course, Dr. Gunn, I hate to see any child begin to hate school," she replied.

A little exploration indicated Janet's skill in word meanings and her vocabulary had remained intact. I couldn't understand why there should be reward given for only one type of skill. Each child is different and should have a chance to show off his unique talents. How about a contest for a couple of weeks based upon vocabulary? The teacher accepted the plan. Luckily, Janet was outstanding in that area and she found new admiration when she showed her skills.

The first student selected the following week, she did beautifully again. Gradually she began to feel accepted, wanted and important. My only hope was that there was not some poor little child that was suffering guilt reactions because of weakness with vocabulary. I did not want to fill my patient list that way!

The manipulation by use of group or team conformity is more widespread in classrooms than is commonly known. I have sat in on many classrooms in my days as a school consultant, only to be appalled. A teacher would let the class know he was ready to start the movie, but, he would add, "We have to wait until one or two of us sit down." Naturally, the other students know who that one or two are. The offending students realize their lack of control hurts not just themselves, but their peers as well.

I recently heard of yet another variation on this ploy. The teacher selected children to report on other children while in the washrooms. If there was noise heard from outside the room and no report given, the spy was in trouble. So the spy was made to feel guilty by his presence and was punished if unacceptable behavior was not reported. (That doesn't seem much different from techniques employed by the Nazis.) The same teacher sometimes had the class as a whole vote on who was causing a disturbance in class. Naturally, the less popular children always tend to "win" this distinction; imagine the guilt of the remainder!

I have heard reports from the children themselves indicating that they hate these techniques. They report feeling constantly guilt-ridden and insecure. They learn to distrust their classmates and often carry vendettas when they believe they have been wronged. One boy admitted to me he lied about a classmate when he had a chance to report that child. He said he was getting back at him but then he felt guilty as a result.

How does one deal with this kind of manipulation? What possible defense is there against it? Well, certainly it would depend upon whom you are. The child is not able to do very much by himself; what he does do will depend upon what messages he receives from his parents. Some parents favor use of these techniques, so as a result, there is little a child can do to help himself.

Recognizing that most children will never read a book like this, I can only give advice to the parents. Some teachers are also open to suggestion, and my hope is that they too will alter their procedures. I believe, though, that we need better selection of teachers. The very harsh teacher with Gestapo methods just cited would do better in another field of endeavor. I can't believe that anyone who treats children as she does really likes and enjoys them. She always looks angry and it is likely that part of this is due to frustration with the job.

Parents can and should become involved in their schools. They need to meet the people who teach their children; fortunately, most teachers will welcome parent conferences. Our tendency is to avoid contact with the school as long as everything is quiet. It is often the silence that spells trouble. Children who are afraid to talk seldom say much about school.

I would invite parents to find out from children about what takes place at school. Given encouragement, children will generally vent their feelings and accurately describe what is happening. When you have a picture from the child, you can then form your own view by meeting the teacher. You can then question her on her goals and techniques.

If something cannot be worked out, you then need to see your principal. Does he agree with the methods used? If not, is he able to do something about it? I would suggest as a parent you try to remain low key. It's unwise to talk too emotionally with those involved with your child's education. I do not recommend an immediate blast of anger. This only precludes free discussion. Think of how you would feel if an "outsider" came into your home or business and blasted the techniques you use.

I feel PTA's and PTO's are excellent organizations through which to act. These organizations can do much to help teachers and thereby make the school days more productive. They can be good information-gathering groups and are useful as sounding boards.

As a last resort, you may need to gather public support and make requests to the superintendent for transfers of teachers. I caution that this is an approach that should be used with care. You do not want to cause all teachers in your system to feel insecure. They won't be effective in that atmosphere. We don't want teachers to be selected merely on a popularity basis. Before you seek removal of a teacher, be sure your reasons are clearly stated. Be sure the teacher is unchangeable and the classroom situation is as bad as you believe it to be.

I have seen some very positive changes take place because of actions by groups of parents working with professionals. One such improvement was in the interests of the hyperactive child (sometimes call hyperkinetic) and those suffering from a learning disability. Once all children like this were made to feel guilty because they couldn't sit still or learn like other children. They were ridiculed both by teachers and students.

Now we recognize their special problems and are taking measures to meet the needs of these children. Probably, we still have much to learn in handling these children. Special remedial classes must not make the child feel unacceptable or "different." For example, there are some techniques wherein the hyperactive child is treated with "stimulus reduction." The theory is that he can't handle extra stimulation because he then becomes overactive. The technique has had some success but one has to be careful that the child does not feel ostracized. I find that children can often understand a program if one explains why in language they can understand. Making them a part of their own remediation program will go a long way towards effective problem management.

It may come as a surprise to learn children are often manipulated because they are rich or poor or black or white. Since I have seen it work that way, I feel it is worth noting.

First, let's talk about the problems of black children. Sometimes they are made to feel inadequate because of their race. Prejudice can be very subtle or very blatant: a teacher may expect less from them than they can give or overtly convey that they are dull. I have even seen the odious approach in which black children are told they have to work extra hard to prove to the world that they can make it.

White children are sometimes told that they have no excuses to offer for their failures. The world accepts them and they have had a rich cultural background. Their parents want them to do well, and if they just exert a little effort, they will obviously succeed.

The economically deprived youngster is often treated like the black child. Since there is a high correlation between the two, the penalty can be severe. They frequently succumb to the pressure and then grow to hate themselves. Some seek punishment for their failures by turning to delinquency. Similarly, I recall one client who was such an inept thief that he always managed to get caught. A little probing evidenced a need to punish himself because he felt so miserable about his failures.

Rich children are sometimes badly handled because of their "cultural advantages." Pressure is applied through manipulation. Like the very bright youngster, they must always do more. In other words, these children are not free to behave like the average child. Set apart, they are pressured unfairly. They look around them and see other children that get massive rewards for much less. In time, many bend under this kind of manipulation and lose interest in school.

What should be done? I don't claim to have all of the answers and I do not feel that this is the proper place to redesign the schools. I do wish we had less in the way of "universal norms," and had guidelines instead. I would like to see more building upon individual needs and abilities, so the learning process was more of a self-fulfilling experience. I wish school could be more fun and involve less pressure.

I believe it can be this way. I have seen examples that prove it. Because my son Billy is very bright, he has had a number of teachers who pushed him to do more than the average child in his class. Billy reacted unfavorably. Then, in second grade, he had a marvelous teacher, Mrs. Ann Schuler, who recognized he could tap his potential.

Mrs. Schuler did not just push for achievement: she explored and soon found that Billy had a very deep interest in dinosaurs. Instead of pushing him to do more reading in general, she gave him the opportunity to do special exploration about his favorite topic. His reading level improved and he loved school.

Mrs. Schuler did similar things with my older boy, Buddy. He is also bright but has a very special kind of perceptiveness about people. Mrs. Schuler allowed him to write about human behavior and interaction in preference to topics like trees or geography. These special projects did wonders for our boys and I can't help but wish we had more Ann Schulers in our school systems!

13

The Loss of Joy Through Guilt

Some folks contend that the New England conscience never prevented people from doing anything; it simply kept them from enjoying it! While this observation is said in jest, clinical evidence suggests that it is true of many people—not just New Englanders.

My own rule is that if something isn't fun, we ought to avoid doing it. Unfortunately, life is rarely this simple. People frequently feel guilty about doing what they really want to do. In fact, situational ambivalence is an important component of guilt reactions. Generally, it's easier to say no than to say yes, anyway; sins of omission are easier to live with than sins of commission.

The first example that comes to mind involves a married couple my wife and I were friends with. The husband was a very successful businessman with a large income. My wife was working at the time and she did not enjoy running home to fix dinner night after night. I frequently worked late, as did our friend, Henry. I have always enjoyed dining out and so did our friends. However, Henry's wife Jan, didn't like eating out. It was hard to tell why; income was no problem and Henry loved it.

Jan mentioned several times that her father was against eating out frequently. He often complained that "a woman's place is in the kitchen." When I first heard that, I commented that it was a shame that her mother cooked so well: she might have easily driven him out to dinner with a few bad meals.

"Oh, but, she wasn't a good cook," Jan retorted. "Dad used to complain all the time!"

When I heard this I realized that our evening out was not going to be easy. Apparently, Jan's father never gave her mother the right to relax and be happy. He viewed dining-out as loafing; cooking was woman's work—a night off was simply irresponsible!

True to form, Jan was a difficult dinner partner. The troubles began long before we decided where we wanted to eat. Everytime a nice restaurant was suggested she objected because it was too "swank" or "extravagant." I will never know how we finally got her to accept our choice. I seem to recall that Henry used her guilt against her by claiming that my wife Vi wanted to go to the one we picked. Much as I disliked that ploy I was grateful that it worked; I seriously wondered if we would starve before a choice was made.

Jan's discomfort increased as we looked over the menu. Everything was "outrageously expensive," but with our assistance she finally placed an order. Though at dinner, she made comments that revealed her guilt. Typical remarks were, "God, I wish I could have ordered the lobster, but I'd never pay that price." And, "At these prices I wish I had stayed home and put the money towards a new dress."

At that point, I also wished that she had stayed home, but I bit my tongue rather than respond. However, think of how Henry felt. Jan's first comment told him that she ordered second best and she really wanted the lobster. She's angry but can't directly show it. With her second statement she slighted Henry's attempt to show her a good time. Jan was abrasive all evening, which points to another problem. No one really enjoys feeling guilt but where do you vent your anger when you feel guilty? You can only punish yourself for so long before you seek out a scapegoat. Jan had a ready target in the three of us, because dining out was our idea. So in her mind, we were the cause of her discomfort.

By the end of the evening Jan's guilt reached its saturation point. If you dine out frequently you will note that restaurant personnel move slowly at the beginning of the meal. With their delaying tactics they hope that the customer will order a huge number of drinks. The latest trend is to wait until you are ready to order food and then suggest wine. Liquor, not food, is where the money is.

Few Americans, however, drink much after dinner. As a result, you will usually find that after you have drunk your limit, service speeds up. The waiter then tries to hustle you out the door to start the routine all over with another party.

This action had a reaction upon Jan. She became nervous and jumpy. Several times she made remarks such as, "I think we really should pay our check and leave, Henry," or "Oh gee, I think we are holding up the table: people are waiting." Finally, everyone became so edgy from Jan's reaction that we decided to leave. Henry invited us back to his house for a night cap. Even that was problematic. Vi and I were having a pleasant conversation with Henry. We did not really want another drink but would have preferred to continue the conversation. We both hate to eat and run. Jan, however, felt quite guilty about causing us to leave early. Consequently, she pushed for the drink to ease her conscience.

I recall other incidents that prove that guilt reactions also affect people when they say yes. Some friends told me recently about people they knew who couldn't relax. They described a situation at a friend's house where they dropped over to borrow some tools. Seems their friend had a rather complete workshop and all they wanted was the loan of a hammer, saw, and screwdriver. Would you believe the saw had to be sharpened before their friend would let them take it?

Or what about the man who can never take a carefree vacation? Many of my clients are like this but one is especially memorable. Bob Johnson was a brilliant stockbroker and, I might add, an incessant worrier. Without his wife, he probably would never have taken a vacation even though he habitually collected travel brochures. He often talked about where he planned to go next year, but next year came and passed, and still no trips.

Finally, one summer, his wife, boss, children and friends all pushed and Bob agreed on a trip to Nassau. Bob would not yield his final agreement, however, until a home was arranged for their family dog. His wife, Jean, did make arrangements, but Bob insisted upon buying overabundant amounts of King's favorite dog food before they left. Seems he had read somewhere that animals feel insecure when they are in a strange household. In retrospect, if that were true it didn't show upon their return. King, 22 pounds overweight, seemed not to want to return home.

Bob and Jean arrived in Nassau a week later than planned. Unfortunately, they arrived on Friday so the Stock Exchange was still open. Immediately upon their arrival Bob began feeling guilty about being away. Now he couldn't watch his accounts. He began to imagine calamities: what if the market suddenly began to drop? With mild irritation, Jean remarked that they were supposed to be on vacation—their first in years. The expectant gleam in her eyes told Bob that she was happy and that he had better not spoil it. He relaxed but only long enough to have one drink. "If I could just find a late newspaper," he thought to himself. But when he inquired, he found that none were available.

"No wonder these islands are so backward," he remarked. "These people don't even follow the world's finances."

"Maybe not," Jean replied, "but they seem much happier than many who do."

Bob took the hint and backed off for a time. But he was still haunted by the absent newspaper. After sitting at the bar with Jean for 10 minutes, he excused himself to go to the men's room. Going by way of the front desk, he found out that there was a newsstand in the heart of town. Needing an excuse to go there, he asked about restaurants. The name of one was provided. When he returned to Jean, he began a great selling job, hoping she would agree to the outing. Jean indicated she preferred to spend a quiet evening in the hotel.

"But honey," Bob pleaded. "They have authentic island food there and we really should try it."

"What sort of food is it exactly?" Jean asked.

"Well it's. . . it's . . . you know."

"What?"

"Oh, it's terrific; you'll love it."

Jean not only allowed herself to be manipulated but also hurried in the time it took her to get dressed. Bob rushed the cab driver, too, all the way to the restaurant. When they arrived, the place looked very disagreeable. Bob assured Jean that it only appeared that way on the outside. He was right——on the inside it looked much worse! Jean was too hungry to leave and agreed to dine there.

"I just hope we don't get sick," she commented as she sat down to order.

Bob paled: that would be just his luck. He might miss a week of market action just at a time when he was sure was going to forge ahead.

Bob made a quick decision on his order and then once again excused himself. He rushed across the street to buy a paper and could hardly wait to get back to the table to check the market news.

I am not even going to describe the scene at the table, but will only leave it to the reader's imagination. That meal set the pace for the whole trip, which ultimately was shortened by three days. The market had gone up on Friday, which was something it had not done in over four days. Bob was filled with guilt because he had not bought into the market as heavily as he felt he should have. He constantly worried about how his "poor clients" would feel seeing the long overdue market rally and not being a part of it.

Jean tried in every way she could to get Bob to relax. Nothing seemed to work, although Bob was better during the weekend. Jean knew that it was only because the market was closed and accurately predicted his return to form on Monday. It seemed to her that every time Bob enjoyed himself, he felt more guilty. Jean got tired of his phrase, so overused, "Here I am having fun while all my clients are losing money." In fact, his clients were probably having more fun than Bob was.

When the market rose on Monday, Bob was at wit's end. His guilt rose accordingly; now two days had passed in which he might have turned a profit. Tuesday was even worse because the market went higher. Finally Jean couldn't take it any longer. She sat down with

Bob and talked about what was happening. She explained that the vacation was not fun for Bob and, as a result, she was having a bad time. She felt they might as well return home. Bob argued but finally agreed.

During the plane ride home, Bob and Jean talked about what the trip had meant to each of them. For his part, Bob made new promises about the future. This time, however, Jean was not having any of it. Somehow she was able to communicate to Bob that he couldn't have fun.

"You know Bob, I honestly believe if you found blowing your nose fun, you would cease and let it drip."

"Am I really that bad?"

"I am afraid so, Bob. You're so bad that I think something has to be done to save our marriage."

Jean later reported that they had talked all night. A few days later, Bob entered therapy. When I first interviewed him, his only motive was "because Jean is unhappy with me." Gradually, as I listened to him, I began to hear more of his own feelings. He became more and more aware of how his tendency to feel guilty intruded on his ability to have fun.

I saw Bob in therapy for little more than a year; during that time he showed remarkable changes in his personality. Much of his conflict originated with a very pushy, excessively hardworking, compulsive but warm father. I think that his personality change came quickly because the mother-son relationship was basically solid and healthy. Bob's father was essentially a nice guy but he was never satisfied with himself. Bob looked up to his father, wanted to please him, and, of course, imitated him. Since the father could not experience joy, the son could not either. I was always suspicious that, underneath the surface, Bob really had greater fear of his father's mother than he knew. She had taken care of him for a very long time when his mother had been ill. From Bob's description, his grandmother was prone to become exceedingly angry when people had fun. She had some sort of saying that the Devil takes over when people have idle hands.

I think perhaps that one of the most gratifying aspects of this case was the change in Jean and in Bob's father. It seems that when his father saw Bob change, he began to feel that perhaps he, too, might experience joy without guilt. Jean called me several years later to report that three generations of men were away fishing. She was most grateful: Bob still worked fairly long hours but he was also able to have fun. He could even take vacations now and certainly enjoyed his family more. Freedom from guilt allowed him to say yes to some very pleasurable things.

There is another kind of guilt reaction that nearly all of us have witnessed. It is typified by the person who says yes to something he wants but then can't bear the burden of having had a good time. Years ago, I worked with a social worker like that. Whenever we traveled to one of the local clinics, he shopped for antiques to furnish his apartment. He was a middle-aged bachelor, with no responsibilities in his life other than himself. So there was no reason for him to feel guilty over his purchases; but he had a knack for finding reasons.

Many of us who had to work with George (as we shall call him) grew tired of his cheapness. He had been fruitlessly searching for an Arabian lamp for over 11 months and whenever he found what he wanted, he balked at the price and never purchased the item. To make matters worse, he finally decided that he needed two lamps because he wished to place them on a pair of night tables. Those of us forced to be around him concluded that this would be an endless search. If one cost too much, how could he bear the expense of two?

One day our traveling clinic visited a small town in southern Illinois. Much to my regret, one of our co-workers told George over lunch that he had seen the much sought-after lamps. When I heard this, I looked up with a mixture of anguish and resentment. However, it was too late. The news was out and our ordeal was beginning.

After he let out a scream that sounded as if he had been stabbed, George immediately asked where and how much. I silently hoped the price would be a thousand dollars each, but no such luck. The damn things were priced dirt cheap but then, George would feel guilty even parting with dirt. Sure enough, after an ulcer-producing lunch, we had to drive to the local store. Since I already had an upset stomach (and being unable to see a grown man cry), I decided to wait in the car. Much to my surprise, George returned to the car in only five minutes carrying a package. Furthermore, he was doing something that was unusual for him: he was smiling. I inferred that our search of nearly a year was over.

In relative peace we drove to the clinic to resume our afternoon schedule. Shortly after we arrived, George turned and said, "I've got something really unusual here, you know what?"

"Let me guess," I retorted, "when you rub the lamp, the owner disappears!"

"Very funny, Dr. Gunn," he shot back. "No, it only cost six dollars."

"What do you mean *it*?" I asked, then immediately wished I hadn't.

The bad news followed. George could not stand to part with $12 so he bought only one, even though he had been searching all this time for a matched pair. Knowing my day was finished, I couldn't wait to deal with the people at the clinic who came for help with real problems.

I was fortunate to escape from George for the remainder of the afternoon, but was less lucky when our clinic team got together for drinks after work. Since our time was limited, it was customary for all of us to discuss our day's cases over a cocktail or two. We usually spent about 1½ hours together and then split up to go our separate ways. However, I knew I would have to suffer with George all through the cocktail hour; by that time I had a hunch I would not feel like eating dinner.

Sure enough, we had just been seated when George began his lamentations.

"Damn, I probably should have bought that other lamp; now it's probably gone."

No one acknowledged the remark: they wouldn't have dared from the way I glared at them. But the silence of others never stopped George.

"Do you think one lamp will look funny by itself?" he

asked——to no one in particular.

"No, George, I think it will be fine; it will stand out better that way," one of the staff said supportively.

"You're just saying that to make me feel better," George shot back. People who enjoy feeling miserable won't let others change their mood.

That whole evening George played his little game. If someone suggested that George should call and place a hold on the other lamp, George complained about spending the other six dollars. It was painful enough to him to have spent six on himself for such a "little non-essential item." He couldn't accept my humor that the "item" was becoming essential to my well being. If anyone supported the idea that one lamp would look good by itself, George accused him of being patronizing.

The whole evening was spent in this way; it certainly wasn't fun. What was particularly funny, though, was that George consumed six drinks because his guilt made him so unhappy. At $1.25 per drink, he spent more money on his bar bill than on the other lamp. But this is the way of the guilt-ridden person. He suffers but he makes everyone else suffer with him. George was a person who couldn't experience joy without guilt. That made him angry and he could not turn his anger upon himself permanently. Ultimately the individual seeks a release of his anger and looks to others for a target. When they try to help, he sabotages their ideas and unleashes his anger upon them. The innocent then suffer greatly.

Very often those with well meaning motivations are whipping boys because they try to help reduce another's guilt reaction. A colleague recalled an illustrative example as I was writing this book. Jane Doe, a friend of his wife's, felt very inadequate about her appearance. She often talked about how "common" her clothes looked and how matronly she always appeared.

Her husband tired of this and took her shopping one day. They went to a very exclusive dress shop and for over an hour she tried on a wide variety of garments. Finally a number of selections were made and her husband assured her that she looked stunning. He was a very supportive husband and was well enough off so that money was not an object. As a matter of fact, Jane's concern never had been money; she could and did easily spend it without any guilt reactions.

The problem came out later that evening when the Does were going out to dine and dance with my colleague and his wife. It was a dress-up occasion, which gave her the opportunity to show herself off. She made a grand entrance when my friends arrived. When they saw her they very supportively said, "Wow."

Now you would think that any person would have hit paradise when she gets that kind of reaction from both men and women. Not Jane, though: her immediate reaction was to look in the mirror to see if she was too flashy. It was reported to me that she stared oddly for nearly 20 seconds. The coaxing of her husband and two friends finally pursuaded her that she looked good. However, most of the evening was spent trying to ease her guilt feelings because Jane couldn't accept the fact that she did indeed, look good. One might summarize her dilemma by saying that there is danger at both ends of the continuum. The person can't afford to fail but be also can't accept too much success. In that situation no one ever knows what to say.

Clothes and overall appearance is a guilt-centered area. It is difficult for many people to establish their own individuality, they may fantasize about attention but aren't comfortable with the reality of it. Few people are sufficiently strong to manage the jealousy of others and their own guilt. I have seen many men who hated their attire but couldn't get rid of them because that was "wasteful."

There is a basic rule of psychology, backed up by many studies, that looking good improves the psyche. Dressing a part means, to some extent, living the part. Research even shows that a person may get ahead in business in part because of the way he looks. Guilt may easily hold him back; it can be used, however, to neutralize this reaction. I have found that many men will modernize their wardrobes if I tell them they owe it to their families. That is called "setting one guilt reaction against another."

Just as some people cannot get rid of something old, there are those that cannot use something new. These people generally do not have a problem about buying things. In fact, they often find that buying is a type of catharsis because it relieves depression. When they feel bored or somewhat restless, they go out and add to their collection of clothes or whatever. Their problem asserts itself when they try to *use* the item they have purchased. Guilt occurs only when there is a chance of joy through use of the item. So they have a whole closet full of new clothes they never use.

This is similar to the person who buys something he likes but can't use it for fear of hurting someone else's feelings. I once knew a lady who had great artistic talent. She painted a lovely oil painting that she had planned to hang over her fireplace. It took her nearly three weeks to complete and, I might add that her husband loved the painting, too. I think that all the time she worked on the painting, (watching it develop with her husband) was like a dream come to fruition. Incidentally, they were a couple who enjoyed doing things to make their home attractive.

A week after she finished it, her aunt sent her a painting that the aunt described as "perfect for your mantle." The trouble was neither the husband nor the wife liked the gift. The wife was just crushed when she saw it, but out of guilt, she felt she had to hang it. Maybe it would have been better to hang the aunt for such a stunt. After all, Auntie knew the painting was in progress. It seemed to me there was a message intended that the younger woman couldn't do anything well. I always felt the husband should have supported his wife in not displaying the aunt's painting. When this couple asked my advice, I suggested returning it to the aunt with the note that it was too beautiful for them to accept. That might indicate they would feel guilty depriving the aunt of such a lovely work of art. They thought about this but couldn't do it; obviously they couldn't tell her the truth, either.

Finally, I call your attention to an even deeper sort of guilt that all of us see from time to time, guilt over the joy of having and expressing feelings. Many people are so afraid to laugh that they can only make strained, choking sounds when they try to express joy. They can't express their anger or even begin to admit feeling angry. Love is hard, too, since they feel unworthy of being loved in return. Theirs is a cautious, unemotional world. They frequently have headaches and disgestive problems. They generally deny all feelings and resort to vicariously living through others.

We might say that loss of joy through guilt is a victimless crime. That has become a popular phrase these days, but is it accurate? I believe that it isn't. Unhappy people are not pleasant to be around. Joyful people are. When an individual feels guilty, he is, in some manner, angry. It is bad enough to turn the anger in word: that hurts one person and deprives others of pleasant company. But, sooner or later, guilt-ridden people punish everyone around them!

My advice would be to simply not allow this to happen. To some extent one can serve as a model for others to emulate. When they see that we experience joy without the need to be punished, they also learn how it can be done. They may say, "I wish I could be as free of guilt as you are." If they do, let them know that you wish they could, too. Maybe you can even talk about how they might move towards such a worthy goal.

In the case of George and his damn lamps, I got to the point where I couldn't take it any longer. I said I wondered whether he didn't need to feel guilty. He thought about that for a time but did not actually answer. That was fine; it was a rhetorical question, anyway. I let him know that it wasn't fun sitting there listening to him complain about how miserable he felt. I did support his ability to carry on more pleasant conversations. When he chose to do that, I would enjoy being with him. When he didn't, I would signal my intentions to leave.

I think that anyone who wished to be constructive with other people can do so, and, at the same time, have more fun themselves. Do not allow others to get your attention by manipulation. Set limits to the amount of time that you will listen to their complaints. Support and thereby reward their mature efforts to handle their guilt feelings.

On the other hand, if the person seems destined to browbeat himself (and you as well) make another kind of decision. Don't feel guilty when you have to say no to their company. There are plenty of enjoyable people in this world; you want to be one of them; pleasant company helps create happy lives. Learn what kinds of things can be done with specific people. Participate along these lines; avoid them when the activity is not fun. If someone can't take a compliment, don't be manipulated into giving one. If a person is fine over lunch but unpleasant on vacations, go to lunch—avoid vacations with them.

Above all, seek those who give you pleasure and avoid those who are unpleasant and want to stay that way. You owe it to yourself, to your family and to the interesting people who are waiting to have the pleasure of your company.

14

Guilt and the World of Work

We would all like to think that, when it comes to the world of work, we operate in a rational or even unemotional manner. Americans pride themselves on their ability to achieve success in business through efficiency. Many business people believe that they coldly operate in an objective manner with only performance as a yardstick.

Actually, emotions play a large part in our daily performance, since the business world is made up of people. I have done much business consultation and have found that guilt is one of the most common emotions. Guilt manipulates business personnel in two main ways. First, it is used by one individual to manipulate others. Secondly, guilt reactions also hamper the individual in self-destructive ways. Therefore, we might say that, in the business world, one individual may be manipulated by his own guilt without the presence of a second party. He may also manipulate or be manipulated by another person.

The first type of guilt reaction is harder to understand but easy to illustrate. I saw a man in therapy who was known to be brilliant, personable and well educated. Yet he never got ahead in the business world. Marshall was 38 and seemed to be happily married. I felt that his solid marriage was a strong asset: at least he did not have to worry about his wife sabotaging him. Marital conflicts deplete a person's energy and, in addition, may send him to the office in a bad mood.

Marshall described to me all of the problems he had getting ahead in the business world. When one of his subordinates did something wrong, Marshall found it difficult to correct him. When called upon to make decisions affecting other people, he was so slow that someone else often had to intervene. When orders came from higher ups it was difficult for Marshall to implement them *if* the directives were going to be unacceptable to others.

I spent some time exploring his business environment. I wanted to see if Marshall was indeed being subtly manipulated by others. From everything Marshall said, he was not. In fact, there were many occasions with subordinates who wanted criticism because they knew they were not doing their jobs correctly. As a further check on my hunch, I talked to Marshall's wife. She turned out to be an immensely supportive woman. As she described the marital interaction, it became apparent she often helped her husband make decisions that he should have been able to make by himself. When pressed she revealed she would have liked for her husband to be more assertive.

Now the picture became clear. Marshall was a man, who in my terminology could not be aggressive or "assertive." Aggressiveness differs from hostility. Thus an aggressive football player tries hard to win but stays within the rules. A hostile football player plays dirty.

Marshall was a guilt-ridden man who had no faith in himself. He was always afraid of making mistakes and offending people. He crumbled whenever anyone gave him the slightest hint of opposition. Other people in his life were not manipulating Marshall; he was doing it to himself.

I decided to use a Rorschach Test to find Marshall's basic personality pattern and how he got that way. I realized I could not plan a course of action until I knew more about Marshall's personality structure and its formation. The Rorschach findings revealed a man who didn't have a truly strong father with whom to identify. His father had been overpowering and crushed him at every turn.

As a boy, Marshall was backed into a corner by his father and forced to make decisions under time pressure. Marshall gave one classic illustration. Because he had loved golf as a boy, he had saved money earned from odd jobs for over half a year to buy a set of clubs. When he asked his dad for help in the purchase of clubs, his dad took him to a golf shop. But his father refused to lend a helping hand. No fatherly advice was ever given.

"Hell, son, you're 11 years old: you have to learn to make your own decision," his father had admonished. Mother tried to help but was told that this was "a man's decision." So, timidly, Marshall selected some clubs that looked attractive to him. The purchase was made, but when Marshall tried to use the new clubs he found they were too light for him. He was simply crushed: he looked at his father in disbelief when he heard his dad say, "Well, son, I knew those shafts were too light, but you wanted them."

There were other similar incidents until Marshall finally began to distrust his own judgement. The father would trap the son in family discussions as well. Whenever Marshall criticized his father, he became hurt and sulked. After a time, Marshall shunned all decision-making and viewed criticism as destructive. His male ego or self-image did not contain elements of aggressiveness.

I felt that intensive therapy might reduce some of the inner guilt but questioned whether it would dramatically increase his aggressiveness. I decided upon another course of action. First, I sent Marshall to an assertiveness training program so that he would become more aggressive. Ultimately, Marshall became involved in several programs with amazing results.

In addition, I did short-term marital counseling aimed at helping the couple work as a team. The wife's job became one of supporting all appropriate changes in her husband's behavior. I came to feel that Marshall was a very lucky man. He had a very supportive wife and she was a great asset in his new development. Interestingly, their very fine marital interaction became even better as Marshall became a stronger, less guilt-ridden person. Within a year Marshall's rise in his company was incredible.

One change that was particularly noticeable regarded decision-making. Marshall no longer acted in such a cautious manner. He learned that no one is perfect: like others, he would make mistakes, but he found he could do his work more quickly. Mistakes could always be corrected later and one could learn from these mistakes. Advice could now be given to others without the fear of failure. As a result, subordinates had a chance to develope their skills, too.

I once experienced a similar type of guilt manipulation whereby one person controls another. An executive of a small company described to me a painful situation he was experiencing. He had hired a friend, John, as a company lawyer. The executive, Max, told me that John and he had been nearly lifelong friends: they were neighbors; played golf together; and had close ties with each other's families.

John was a capable lawyer but was constantly overworked. He could not say no to anyone and he didn't know how to schedule his work. Consequently there were times when he simply did not get important jobs done. He promised but he didn't follow through.

When I suggested that John sounded a bit irresponsible, Max winced. He began to make excuses, insisting he didn't want John's feelings hurt. He said he couldn't bear to fire him.

"What does John say when you ask him why some job is not finished?," I asked.

"Well, let's see," he replied. "Oh I guess, mostly he tells me how busy he is, that he meant to get at it, and how sorry he is. Most of the jobs I give him are little and probably don't pay much but he does them because we are such good friends."

So now I knew. Max was being manipulated by guilt feelings. He couldn't look realistically at a situation when a friend was involved. If John had been a good friend, he would have told Max that he just couldn't handle the quantity of work Max sent him. Instead he used manipulation by guilt which effectively obscured Max's view of the situation.

There was an easy solution that could solve the company's problem and still preserve the friendship. Like it or not, John had to go. I instructed Max to take John out for a long lunch. He was to tell John how much he liked his work and that he had much more for him. It all had to be done quickly but he was sure John could handle it. Max was to list as many jobs as possible for John to do. "Give him everything you can conceivably find. Tell him you know it will be hard but you are sure he can handle it."

"Then when you get back to your office, see if you can find a couple of more jobs for John every day. Have your secretary call constantly with more work and to see how everything is going. Take up as much of John's office time as possible. Always congratulate him but add more work."

Max smiled and agreed to the program. John lasted less than a week. In fact, Max reported back after their lunch that John had immediately had reservations about his added duties. Three days later John asked Max out for lunch. He wanted to know if some of the work could be shifted to someone else. Max said no, he liked John's work and did not want two company lawyers. Max was pleased about the chance for lunch because he had yet more work for John. The following day John came to Max's office. He was sorry but he had to resign: he couldn't handle all the extra work. Max was very "understanding" and allowed John to step aside gratefully.

Generally speaking, the guilt-ridden boss is not an easy person to work for. Seldom delegating authority, he instead feels that he must do everything himself. When he does give some responsibility to another person, he never actually lets go. This type of individual seems to believe that he is the only one who can do anything well. At the same time, however, he is never satisfied with his performance.

In theory, it might sound as if the guilt-ridden superior ought to be easy to work for. After all, some would argue, he will do your work for you. This is clearly undesirable because how will you get to show your talents and rise in the company? Secondly, let us recall that those who feel guilty push others to ease their discomfort. They will do extra work but will constantly complain about it.

Robert S. approached me for advice about his superior, Walter M., who was just a constant griper. Robert was highly ambitious and wanted to advance into the executive ranks of his rather large company. Walter was his immediate superior and constantly griped, "I have to do everything myself." When Walter made an error, he blamed Robert as well as all of those under him. Work in the department lagged and reflected on everyone. In addition, Robert had the feeling that Walter did not want him to look really outstanding. To do so might mean that Robert would eventually outrank Walter.

I suggested that Robert not allow himself to be so manipulated. First he needed to have a clear definition of his duties. Once that was spelled out, he was to hold these duties and to surrender them only when Walter specifically ordered him to do so. This could be accomplished in several ways.

For instance, if Walter began complaining about the work of his subordinates, Robert was to very specifically ask if he had done something wrong. If Walter answered yes, then Robert should ask sufficient questions so that he understood his shortcomings. He could learn from that type of critical appraisal. Robert could also then inform Walter that he knew how to correct his errors. After he had done so, he was to bring the work back to Walter for approval. In this way, Robert would be removing Walter's excuses for taking over jobs.

I suggested that this might be a type of smoke screen to prevent a rash of criticisms. Walter was just looking for an excuse to take away delegated jobs. By making many criticisms, he is, in effect, saying, "There is too much to be corrected."

Robert was instructed to recognize the tactic and then ask Walter to spell out his criticisms. He was to take the weaker ones first and indicate that it would be helpful if these could be explained further. I told him to try to make the point that you appreciate that he wants to help you. Chances are he will soon realize he is on very shaky ground and will drop the minor criticism.

What the victim of the manipulation is actually doing is forcing the manipulator to get specific. Instead of

being frightened off by guilt feelings, the victim is saying something positive. He can handle criticism and he
is able to remove the block to being given his appropriate duties. By requesting that the vague complaints be
turned into a specific criticism, one can examine the situation reasonably.

I said earlier that there were two strategies that Robert might use to control Walter. Suppose Walter refused
to make specific criticisms for taking back duties that
were rightfully Robert's. The attempt on Walter's part to
manipulate should still be brought into the open. Robert
must not quietly accede to authority with the tacit guilt
that everyone under Walter is inadequate. Someone
hired all of these people: if they are inadequate, then
so is the judgment of the person who selected them.
When an employee passively accepts his loss of authority, he is tacitly stating that he accepts his limitations.
Instead make it clear who has made the decision to
take the job over. In this case, it was Walter. A reply
such as, "Well, then sir, do I understand that you wish
to take over this project?"

Now Walter has to accept the clear responsibility for
his decision. Soon the top people began to wonder
what was wrong with him. They called him in to find out
what the stumbling block was. After a discussion, he
was told to train Robert to do the jobs he was supposed to do or else be replaced by someone who could.
As Robert began to have more freedom to do his work,
he began to assert himself. His record was good and
he began his move upwards.

All of us have at one time or another wanted an appointment with someone who was difficult to reach.
Usually we encounter a secretary who seems to earn
her salary by keeping people away from her boss.
Should you ask when you might see this person, you
are likely to get a reply that indicates she surely
wouldn't know but can find someone else to help you.
When you press your case, you are continually put off.
I have occasionally detected the insinuation that I was
asking a stupid question.

Intimidation is enforced by guilt; many people are put
off by an approach in which they are made to feel

guilty. The secretary conveys the impression that you are asking something unreasonable of her. I have short patience with this kind of situation and have always persisted. I ask: "If you can't tell me when your boss will be available, please refer me to someone who can." Generally the secretary reacts to this. You are now implying that you may have to go over her head to get information that she should be able to provide. This is tantamount to declaring to others that she is incompetent.

Once I met heavy opposition from a secretary who greatly irritated me. Having wasted enough time in conversation, I decided the most economical path to follow was a letter. I wrote indicating that I had tried to secure an appointment; that I felt no one else would be able to handle my problem; but that the secretary could not give me a possible convenient time. As I expected, the secretary called me after opening her boss's mail.

Some of the readers may feel that I am hard on secretaries who try to perform their duties. I wish to explain why. I have come to feel that they arbitrarily screen their boss's calls and make decisions that they should not be making. This insight resulted from a discovery. I called once asking to speak with an administrative official of a company. I was asked my name and, due to a poor connection, spelled it out. I was immediately told that the person was not in.

Thinking nothing further of it, I said, "Okay, would you ask Mr. Smith to call Dr. Gunn when he gets back."

"Oh, *Doctor* Gunn, well just a minute, I think I might be able to reach him."

Why in the world should the title "Doctor" have carried so much weight? If the boss really was out earlier, why not now? Maybe I should have said I was the Director of Internal Revenue to save even more time. I concluded that plenty of manipulation was going on and that some bosses aren't aware of it.

There is one area of manipulation by guilt that is known to every woman in business. I refer to the subtle implication that the individual applying for a position is suspect because she is a woman. It is difficult to defend against this attitude because so much is left unsaid. When the personnel man asks, "What are your qualifications?" the woman applying immediately goes on the defensive. Sometimes she may be asked if she is applying for a permanent position. The unspoken meaning is that you may be planning to work only as long as it takes you to trap a man into marriage.

What differences does this all make if the woman is finally hired? Plenty, I think. First of all, if the lady feels guilty because she dared to enter a man's world, she is bargaining from weakness. She feels inadequate and will probably work for less money than she deserves. She therefore broadcasts her dissatisfaction and vulnerability to her employers.

That will make a great difference in her future. When one becomes typecast, it is very difficult to change one's image. First impressions generally persist past personality changes. If a woman is to advance to a higher, more responsible position, she must generate confidence and aggressiveness. It is most difficult to reflect either one if a person feels guilty about her very existence.

Most people develop an image at work. It is very difficult to continue working at a job when one feels unaccepted. It is particularly frustrating if you can't change the cause of the rejection.

Women in business face great obstacles. There are some men who are loath to giving a woman a chance. These men feel threatened whenever a female does something as well or better than they. However, that is a defect in their male egos that women need not feel responsible for. They must refuse to feel guilty and assertively move toward their goal.

Many companies, even in this day and age are simply not going to give a woman a chance. If you feel apologetic (and guilt-ridden) because you are a woman, you succumb to their backwardness. In actuality, the world does not end when you take such a job. You begin your search, and what becomes significant is that you have a launching pad for new job search.

A prospective new employer may ask why you are

applying for a position at his company. You can honestly state that it is because of your desire to get ahead. If
that statement appeals to him, you then have an indication that he is what you want as a boss. If not, then
you have found another "chauvinist pig" and employment there won't be any better.

There are a variety of situations in a work setting
that can be dealt with here. They essentially involve
manipulation by guilt in assigning work responsibility.
For example, when a subordinate is requested to get
some work done, he may indicate an unwillingness to
do so. He responds by suggesting that he is already
overworked. I have seen situations where the higher
level worker backs off and does the work himself. He
has increased his own work load because he was manipulated, and in the future he will hesitate to ask the
manipulator for help.

Of course, the corollary to that is the subordinate
who is manipulated into doing jobs that should not be
his. In all of these situations, I believe that reality
should be the guide. Try to get everything out in the
open. Spell out what your duties are or ask that they
be spelled out. It does not hurt to say that you understood your duties as such and such; ask if there has
been either a misunderstanding or a change.

Generally, when such definitions are made, we find
that most people have some flexibility. They can negotiate job duties. On the other hand, when you allow yourself to be manipulated you will grow to hate your job.
That will cause your work to fall off sooner or later.
When people find that you cannot be manipulated, they
will generally take a more rational tack. They will communicate openly, foresaking manipulation by guilt.

15

Exploitation by Guilt:
The Political Arena

When I first discussed this book with friends, they found it easy to see how guilt related to personal problems. But guilt and manipulation by government? No, there they drew the line. I suspect they felt that I had become somewhat paranoid. Some said the government can cause anxiety and maybe even depression, but not guilt. Then, as we talked, they began to change their minds. I think the reader will see why.

First of all, let us remember that government is simply made up of a group of people who are paid out of the public purse. As political creatures, they must try to sell the electorate on a plan of action. In a sense, they are constantly on trial: if we decide we do not like their policies, they are generally shunted out of office. In that sense, I believe politicians are salesman; instead of products, they sell politics.

I have no quarrel with any of the process that I have just described. I do take issue with the way political campaigns are conducted. People will use whatever works; in the heat of a political campaign a candidate will often resort to what works *quickly*. A democracy is based upon an enlightened public, however. No country will remain a democracy very long if its people do not vote rationally. I feel that today we are often in danger of voting away our rights. In public opinion polls I often notice that what the people want on key issues is very different from what the government does.

Why is there such a gap? I am certainly not going to make a case for guilt as the sole factor. There are many reasons that are beyond the scope of this book. But I do believe guilt plays a very big part. I think we can begin to see how when we talk about the election process. Let's take a look at some of the maneuvering that has been done on the national level.

When John Kennedy ran for government, his Catholic background was a subject of controversy. It was raised as an issue, nicely dealt with and seemingly dismissed. Then it seemed to find its way back into the campaign as the Democrats revived it as an issue. Over and over again, someone backing Senator Kennedy would raise the issue and then declare that it ought *not* to be an issue. You may remember the phrase that "if a Catholic could fight for his country in time of war, he should be able to run for president."

Many years after Senator Kennedy was elected, it was revealed some members of his staff had gathered significant information via a public opinion poll. Things had changed since the days when another Catholic candidate had run for President. Now there was a national guilt reaction; any hint that prejudice had an effect produced a counter-reaction. All the evidence gathered suggested that guilt reactions would cause people to switch their vote. In a close election, that could handily make a difference.

Guilt has been used at the national level, too. People have been manipulated to feel they needed to vote for a particular man lest the country be "weak." I think many people can still recall the "missile gap." We were told that a previous administration had allowed the Russians to get ahead of us in the armament race. Sure, increased defense expenditures would cost us more money, but who among us would sell our country short? Who wanted America to become a second-rate country? This approach gave rise to a spirit of nationalism which manipulated us through guilt. Ironically, years later, it appeared that this "missile gap" was imaginary.

When Senator Goldwater ran for President, guilt made a comeback. It was used on both sides. Senator Goldwater's backers used the phrase: "In your heart you know he's right." Any number of people consequently told me they felt guilty because they wanted to vote for President Johnson.

On the other side, Senator Goldwater was accused of irresponsibility. By advocating such drastic steps as the escalation of the Viet Nam war, he might precipitate the breakout of total war. Suddenly, those who backed Senator Goldwater felt guilty because their man might do something to bring about the slaughter of hundreds of thousands of young men. Horrible descriptions of what war was like ensued. It mattered little that we had been involved in that unfortunate war for some time. Suddenly there was manipulation by guilt. What seems interesting in retrospect is that many of the moves suggested by Senator Goldwater were later followed.

Not only at the national level is guilt utilized as a means of vote manipulation. Those who are running for Congress generally claim they are for the people of some particular region—be it a state or portion of a state. Everyone else is against that region or favors "wasting money" for some unworthy project. Thus in the coal mining regions, a candidate will claim his opponents are ruled by the oil companies; in manufacturing regions, the claim will be that labor influenced his opponents, etc. The argument is nearly always the same.

Frequently, too, there is a battle between the President and Congress. The President needs to keep the people as a whole satisfied while Senators and congressmen have to keep their constituents pleased. When the President doesn't get what he wants, he claims we have a "do-nothing Congress." He hopes to manipulate them into falling into line. Usually the Congressmen indicate that one should not back the President because to do so would be to give him too much power or to spend too much money.

When a President takes office, he must still be very concerned about public opinion. He needs to keep the people in his corner. There are times when a president pushes hard to sell an unpopular idea. Some of you may recall this during the Viet Nam War. The war seemed to drag on forever at an enormous cost. Vice-President Humphrey went on a speaking tour when he tried to convince people that more money was needed

in order to win the war. (I believe it was called a "sur-
tax.") At one point, Mr. Humphrey said: "It's only a thin
dime out of a dollar; who would miss that?" The approach seems to me one of manipulation by guilt. When
someone asks for a dime in that manner, people often
feel guilty for refusing. It seems as if so little is being
asked for that we would be stingy if we refused.

Actually, Mr. Humphrey was not asking for a dime.
He was asking for 10 percent of every thousand, or
worse yet, a thousand out of every ten thousand dollars. It should also be remembered this was not the
only tax we were expected to pay. Mr. Humphrey was
successful in obtaining funds; yet the war went on.

Then Mr. Nixon came into the White House, dedicat-
ed to ending the war honorably. Guilt reactions were
again used. Who would dare stand up and say they
wanted the war ended *without* honor? Meanwhile the
war raged: many more men lost their lives and the cost
escalated.

Of course, then came Watergate. I have a hunch that
guilt reactions played a part on both sides of the
Watergate hearings. This statement is not meant to diminish the tragedy of Watergate nor its apparent injustice. But I think there is evidence that other politicians
were also guilty of wrongdoing. Very often people deal
with their own guilt feelings by casting an indignant fin-
ger at someone else.

At any rate, Mr. Nixon claimed for a long time that
he was being picked on. He insisted that he had given
all the facts and was not trying to cover up anything.
He used humor more than he ever did in his earliest
political days, seemingly working on the image of a
"nice guy." At one point, he said something to the effect that some may wish to mire in the mud of Watergate but many Americans wanted to go on to bigger
things. Thus, those wanting to get at the truth were ob-
sessed with trivia. As we all know, these defensive approaches failed.

Before I leave the political arena, I want to mention
two ploys used at election time. One is the free ride to
the polling place. Let's say that you accept a ride from
the Republicans. Can you still say thanks to these

"nice guys" and vote against them? It is possible that they know that your guilt may work for them. Secondly, what about the political donation? It seems that money is usually requested with the statement that a particular man needs the money in order to preserve our great country. If you don't contribute, you have failed your country. Who could refuse?

There are many other areas where I have felt guilt reactions have played a big part. I wonder, for example, about our welfare system. We certainly do put a lot of money into the various programs but I have doubts as to how well they work. In the past, I have acted as a consultant to some of the programs. I noted one very big shortcoming. Many of the social workers felt that they as middle-class people were somehow guilty because the poor never got very far. I seemed to me it was internal guilt caused by being successful.

What did that do to the programs? Well, instead of helping poor people help themselves become successful, they were encouraged to be failures. Instead of counseling people to train themselves more adequately and find better jobs, they were told how to get public aid. The workers felt sorry for the poor: they did not try to help them earn more money. When women continued to have children out of wedlock, they were given sympathy and money. Seldom did anyone relay to these women about how to avoid future pregnancies.

I noticed how the poor reacted to these programs and I was generally impressed with their reactions. Oh sure, there were a few who relished the greater attention and used the system. But the majority were angry: they wanted to get somewhere and usually were not helped to do so. Many quit going for help and fell back into the wasteful system. Some would no longer even avail themselves of free medical attention.

A psychologist cannot help but wonder about many aspects of our foreign policy. Very often we go from one extreme to another. First, we are very angry with some country: we denounce them, and place travel and trade restrictions on them. Then all of a sudden we start talking about that country in a different light. They go from bad to good guys overnight. But, along with that we start giving loans and gifts. Boy, do we give gifts. Is it possible that we feel guilty because of our first action? Do we now have to doubly make it up to them?

In addition, it seems that when we have a friendly nation, we worry all the time that we may lose them. With those nations we also give gifts by the score. If they vote against us in the UN, we worry that perhaps some break in our relationship has taken place. It is as if we feel unworthy—and that, of course, is guilt. Therefore, we believe ~ooner or later we will be found wanting.

On the receiving end, we ask: do countries who depend upon us possibly suffer from guilt? Could they dislike the fact that we do too much for them? Does the guilt produce an unwanted dependency? Is it not possible that their guilt ultimately produces a kind of rebellion? It must be remembered that people don't like this uncomfortable feeling of guilt and they can rebel.

I personally believe that guilt plays a very big part of our whole income tax picture. In this area, the dynamics are very complicated and emotions other than guilt play a part. First, we all want to be successful: our prestige and our tax collector require it. But, the more successful we are, the more we pay. At tax time, we have to feel guilty for having been successful unless, of course, we cheat. If we do, though, we will feel both guilt and anxiety.

The government plays a game with us. They tell us that we should take every possible deduction coming to us. They will even give us advice on how to do it. Be careful, though, not to go over the line. Do that and their clever computers will catch you. So the challenge is on. Sometimes we get into gray areas. We will feel incompetent if we don't search out all possible deductions and scared if we do it too well.

As a psychologist, I have little advice to offer in the governmental area. We use psychologists in war time to fight an enemy, but in peace time I have not seen much use of the psychological profession for government consultation. Maybe that is because we can't be drafted. Maybe it is felt that we only know how to work against people. If so, we all suffer from our negative image. I don't see much chance of changing government policy. I do feel that something can be done at the grass roots level by changing people. As we all operate more rationally, perhaps we will select better people to rule us—that is, if we can find them. Perhaps we will demand more of government and refuse to be manipulated.

16
The Guilt-Ridden Personalities:
Basic Types

By this time it should be clear that there are certain basic personality types which characteristically use guilt to manipulate. It seems appropriate here to profile and classify these types—many of whom I'm sure you'll recognize.

Men: Boyfriends, Husbands, Fathers

The guilt-ridden man is rigid: he relies on a single technique to manage most interpersonal situations. He demands attention implicitly but never states his needs outright. A habitual complainer, he attempts to manipulate others into making decisions for him. Convinced that his judgment is faulty, he lacks confidence. While he is generally timid in dealing with most moderately aggressive men, he is very likely to bully those who appear weak. In all likelihood, he has problems handling anger since recognizing this emotion produces guilt. Usually he contains these feelings until they surface— as volatile eruptions.

As a boyfriend, the guilt-ridden male is bad news. He is continually jealous, requiring the exclusive attention of his girlfriend. Usually he is ambivalent about sex. Readily transferring his guilt to his partner, he is often boastful about his "performance."

Because of his preoccupations, he is unable to give fully when he does get involved in a relationship.

Guilt-ridden husbands are even more of a menace to their wives. Worrying constantly about the advances of other men, they vociferously attack "Don Juans," of whom, in reality, they are envious. They are generally afraid of liberated women but may often complain of their wives being cold. Characteristically demanding attention, they negotiate from a position of weakness. In general, they have had difficulty in separating from their parents, especially their mothers. As a consequence,they often compare their wives unfavorably to their mothers.

As fathers, the guilt-ridden male worries continually about his adequacy. In practice they either neglect their children wholesale or shower them with unwanted attention.

Male children become vehicles for thwarted ambition: girls, on the other hand, are smothered. Communication about sex is often difficult. Discipline is established in a haphazard fashion, frequently seesawing between extremes. In retaliation, their children become adept at manipulating them and thus miss out on appropriate parental guidance.

Women: Girlfriends, Wives, Mothers

The guilt-ridden woman mismanages feelings of anger in a similar fashion. A common ploy is the "passive hostile approach," or silent treatment as we commonly know it. She reacts through nonreaction. Generally passive, she is easily taken advantage of, but makes much of her martyrdom.

In romantic relationships, they are markedly inhibited. Often they will put conditions on their sexual favors in order to manipulate their boyfriends. Anxious and demanding, they cling to their boyfriends and usually do not initiate careers. Like their male counterparts, they are generally dependent and dominated by their parents, especially their mothers. They are also quick to criticize the behavior of female peers.

The guilt-ridden wife is unable to be joyful, sensual and sexually spontaneous. Envious of her husband's openess (unless he is equally guilt-ridden), she is jealous of attention he receives from anyone else. Inhibition of all emotion is punctuated by periodic outbursts. The guilt ridden-wife finds it hard to be assertive, and constantly complains of being taken advantage of. Overall, she is fearful and dependent.

As a mother, the guilt-ridden woman is overprotective and worries constantly that tragedy will befall her children. Frightened of sex and anger, she punishes whenever children display interest in these areas. She has many problems establishing parental authority, vacillates between rigidity and complete control. When tested by her children, she doesn't follow through. She is dependent upon her own children, and tends to give many double messages.

Children: Adolescents and Young Adults

The guilt-ridden child is a timid, fearful person who clings to his parents in the hopes that they will accept him. Prone to bad dreams, he is afraid of teachers and other authority figures and he lacks spontaneity. He is afraid of aggressive children and he bullies children more fearful than he.

When the guilt-ridden child becomes an adolescent, aberrations of behavior become pronounced in two directions. The prototypical rebel without a cause, he may identify with unpopular causes just to get even with authority figures. A problem child endeavors to be free, but in reality, lacks authenticity.

Other adolescents who are guilt-ridden become fearful, reserved, withdrawn, and inhibited. This group is linked to the rebel in ways that may not seem obvious. Both groups worry a lot, are afraid of their impulses, and are emotionally inhibited. One group reacts explosively, the other is subdued. But neither group rationally express emotion.

What makes the guilt-ridden young adult distinctive? Generally a struggle over dependency upon others with this person. He or she finds himself suddenly on his own. They worry a great deal about survival. They have nagging self-doubts and they frequently become extensive conformists in the hope of fitting in. Since it is generally difficult for them to be assertive it becomes most difficult to find their place in the sun.

Employer, Worker, Community

People, the Religious Leader

As you might expect, a guilt-ridden boss is difficult to work for and with. He hates to make decisions and constantly changes his mind. Leaning upon others for support, he never delegates authority. He is glaringly inconsistent: one moment he asks someone to do something for him and the next minute he complains about the result. Above all, he doesn't trust anyone, including himself.

Guilt-ridden workers are similarly afraid of making any decisions. They lack initiative and constantly seek direction from others. Even then they require frequent reclarification of instructions. Often they complain about never getting ahead but they never demonstrate executive ability. They may be very loyal but only because of fear. To their credit, these workers do often work (excessively) long hours but generally their labors are unproductive. Lacking personal freedom, they fail to develop creativity.

Guilt-ridden workers in the service professions have two chief characteristics. They want to reform everyone; and, they want to change the world without knowing why. Unfortunately, they often choose as target people who do not want to be changed. Their attitude is one of "I know what is really good for you." Much of what these workers suggest doesn't work because they are too theoretical and not inclined to modify theories in light of practice. They give too much of themselves and exhaustedly complain that the world changes too slowly.

When a guilt-ridden person becomes a religious leader, he generally transfers his guilt to everyone with whom he works. He is severe and unrelenting towards others; basically he doesn't trust human nature, is afraid of most emotional impulses, is adept at making others feel guilty and is rigid and overly conventional.

Seldom popular, joyful or creative, the guilt-ridden person is extremely resistant to forms of growth. As we have determined in our study of personality types, the "power" of the guilt-ridden person lies chiefly in his ability to manipulate.

17
To Be or Not to Be Manipulated

So now it is up to you. You've seen how every area of our lives is subject to manipulation. There are two major questions that everyone needs to answer.

First, I'd like to ask whether you want to be manipulated by your guilt feelings? If you allow it to happen, others will surely manipulate you this way. Shopping with a friend the other day, I witnessed the common occurrence of manipulation in action. He asked a salesperson for help. She replied, "You will have to wait until I finish adding my receipts." Her tone implied, "How dare you disturb me!"

My friend apologized and stood around waiting. I couldn't help commenting that apparently *his* time was expendable: it was okay for him to waste his time waiting. That was all that it took; my friend asked if there was someone else who could wait on him. He indicated that his time was valuable, too. The salesperson decided that she could add up her receipts later.

I repeat that it is up to you: the first step is always to look at yourself. If you get your guilt feelings under control, no one will be able to manipulate you through guilt. It's unreasonable to expect the world to change for you. People will continue to use whatever they find works with you. But if you change your behavior, you'll undoubtedly find that other people will react differently towards you!

The second question I ask is whether you wish to manipulate other people through their guilt feelings. There may be some justification for employing this practice in business with people who seemingly can't be handled any other way. In general, though, manipulation through guilt feelings doesn't improve human interaction significantly. Don't allow others to manipulate you, but seek for more constructive interaction where ever possible. Try to promote growth in everyone, including yourself. I suggest that you support that which is constructive and eliminate negative influences.

If problems persist, you have many options by which help can be obtained. There are many psychotherapeutic approaches that can help you deal more effectively with guilt feelings. In addition, there are assertive training courses, marital counseling clinics, and a variety of guilt and anxiety reduction programs that may also be helpful. Remember to focus on your feelings; they will guide you in making the most important changes.

It is my hope that this book has helped you to think about your behavior and how you interact with people. I invite you now to check your new self-image after having read this book. It might be fun to also invite a friend, spouse, or parent to take the following test with you. Then compare your results on the two quizzes. Be prepared for some informative changes, and good luck!

Quiz

Instructions: Answer whether you agree or disagree with these statements on your attitudes, behavior, experience, or personality. Use the question mark only if you are absolutely unsure of how to decide. Answers will follow the questions.

	Agree	?	Disagree
1.) I hate to ever let anyone down.	☐	☐	☐
2.) I have bad dreams at least once a week.	☐	☐	☐
3.) I am constantly dieting.	☐	☐	☐
4.) I do not have many nervous habits.	☐	☐	☐
5.) I have frequent headaches.	☐	☐	☐
6. I have not had a vacation in two years.	☐	☐	☐
7.) One should work hard at everything one does.	☐	☐	☐
8.) I never make foolish purchases.	☐	☐	☐
9.) It upsets me to feel angry.	☐	☐	☐
10.) It upsets me when someone gets angry with me.	☐	☐	☐
11.) I am very influenced by advertising.	☐	☐	☐
12.) I usually want the same things as other people.	☐	☐	☐
13.) Happy people are successful people.	☐	☐	☐
14.) I worry about my health.	☐	☐	☐
15.) I don't like public disagreements.	☐	☐	☐

	Agree	?	Disagree
16.) I do not usually fill out mailed questionaires.	☐	☐	☐
17.) There is nothing wrong with high pressure sales techniques.	☐	☐	☐
18.) It is very hard to find privacy.	☐	☐	☐
19.) It is difficult for me to ask for what I want.	☐	☐	☐
20.) I hate to throw anything away.	☐	☐	☐
21.) I have given up smoking many times.	☐	☐	☐
22.) I get excited at sporting events.	☐	☐	☐
23.) I am an enthusiastic person.	☐	☐	☐
24.) It is inexcusable to lose one's temper.	☐	☐	☐
25.) When things go well, I know they are bound to go badly later.	☐	☐	☐
26.) I have at least one hobby and regularly spend time with it.			
27.) My judgment is often quite poor.	☐	☐	☐
28.) I hold in many of my feelings.	☐	☐	☐
29.) I readily admit my faults.	☐	☐	☐
30.) People often borrow things from me.	☐	☐	☐
31.) I can talk out my anger.	☐	☐	☐
32.) People say I give advice too readily.	☐	☐	☐
33.) I am often indecisive.	☐	☐	☐
34.) Seeing others fail makes one feel they are not alone.	☐	☐	☐

	Agree	?	Disagree
35.) I am a highly individual person.	☐	☐	☐
36.) I often find myself doing things I don't want to do.	☐	☐	☐
37.) I love to take on responsibility.	☐	☐	☐
38.) I back off in most arguments.	☐	☐	☐
39.) It is difficult to argue with someone who is smarter than I am.	☐	☐	☐
40.) I should read more than I do.	☐	☐	☐
41.) I generally maintain a neat appearance.	☐	☐	☐
42.) It is difficult to stop someone else's anger.	☐	☐	☐
43.) Sometimes it is fun to just do nothing.	☐	☐	☐
44.) I am always trying to improve the world.	☐	☐	☐
45.) I frequently take a drink when offered even though I don't want it.	☐	☐	☐
46.) People are always giving me advice.	☐	☐	☐
47.) I am a meticulous person.	☐	☐	☐
48.) It disturbs me to be wrong.	☐	☐	☐
49.) I derive personal satisfaction from my accomplishments.	☐	☐	☐
50.) I am easily embarrassed.	☐	☐	☐

For Women Only

	Agree	?	Disagree
1.) My parents made most of my decisions for me.	☐	☐	☐
2.) I have good sexual relationships.	☐	☐	☐
3.) There are many acceptable moral codes for sexual behavior.	☐	☐	☐
4. I am fixed in my sexual values.	☐	☐	☐
5. I can comfortably talk to some men about sexual matters.	☐	☐	☐
6.) Men have a totally unfair position in the world today.	☐	☐	☐
7.) I was a troublesome child.	☐	☐	☐
8.) I could usually talk to my parents.	☐	☐	☐
9.) My parents usually expressed confidence in me.	☐	☐	☐
10.) I am different from my parents in a number of ways and they accept this fact.	☐	☐	☐

For Men Only

	Agree	?	Disagree
1.) My parents made most of my decisions for me.	☐	☐	☐
2.) I have good sexual relationships.	☐	☐	☐
3.) There are many acceptable moral codes for sexual behavior.	☐	☐	☐

	Agree	?	Disagree
4.) I am fixed in my sexual values.	☐	☐	☐
5.) I can generally talk to women about sexual matters.	☐	☐	☐
6.) I think women have too much power.	☐	☐	☐
7.) I was a troublesome child.	☐	☐	☐
8.) I could usually talk to my parents.	☐	☐	☐
9.) My parents generally expressed confidence in me.	☐	☐	☐
10.) My parents accept the fact that I am different from them in a number of ways.	☐	☐	☐

For Those Under 25

	Agree	?	Disagree
1.) My parents make most of my decisions for me.	☐	☐	☐
2.) I can accept my sexual feelings.	☐	☐	☐
3.) There is more than one acceptable moral code for sexual behavior.	☐	☐	☐
4.) My sexual views often change.	☐	☐	☐
5.) I can comfortably talk about sex with some people.	☐	☐	☐
6.) I find it hard to communicate with the opposite sex.	☐	☐	☐
7.) I can never repay my parents.	☐	☐	☐
8.) I was described as a "good baby."	☐	☐	☐
9.) I can usually talk to my parents.	☐	☐	☐
10.) My parents never seemed to understand me.	☐	☐	☐

Quiz Answers

The answers to the questions appear below and each question has a different point value. Note the points assigned to each answer. If the answer is correct, you receive the total point value of the answer: if incorrect, you receive no points. Add your total score and rate yourself on the self-rating scale.

Answers	Points	Answers	Points
1.) Disagree	4	14.) Disagree	3
2.) Disagree	5	15.) Disagree	2
3.) Disagree	1	16.) Agree	1
4.) Agree	5	17.) Disagree	1
5.) Disagree	5	18.) Disagree	6
6.) Disagree	3	19.) Disagree	7
7.) Disagree	2	20.) Disagree	2
8.) Agree	1	21.) Disagree	1
9.) Disagree	7	22.) Agree	3
10.) Disagree	8	23.) Agree	6
11.) Disagree	2	24.) Disagree	6
12.) Disagree	2	25.) Disagree	3
13.) Agree	4	26.) Agree	2

Answers	Points	Answers	Points
27.) Disagree	5	39.) Disagree	3
28.) Disagree	10	40.) Disagree	1
29.) Agree	2	41.) Agree	2
30.) Disagree	3	42.) Disagree	3
31.) Agree	7	43.) Agree	2
32.) Disagree	3	44.) Disagree	1
33.) Disagree	10	45.) Disagree	6
34.) Disagree	2	46.) Disagree	5
35.) Agree	10	47.) Disagree	2
36.) Disagree	3	48.) Disagree	2
37.) Agree	2	49.) Agree	7
38.) Disagree	4	50.) Disagree	5

For Women Only

	Answers	Points
1.)	Disagree	12
2.)	Agree	10
3.)	Agree	10
4.)	Disagree	10
5.)	Agree	10
6.)	Disagree	5
7.)	Disagree	10
8.)	Agree	10
9.)	Agree	12
10.)	Agree	10

For Men Only

	Answers	Points
1.)	Disagree	12
2.)	Agree	10
3.)	Agree	10
4.)	Disagree	10
5.)	Agree	10
6.)	Disagree	5
7.)	Disagree	10
8.)	Agree	10
9.)	Agree	12
10.)	Agree	10

For Those Under 25

	Answers	Points
1.)	Disagree	12
2.)	Agree	10
3.)	Agree	10
4.)	Agree	10
5.)	Agree	10
6.)	Disagree	5
7.)	Disagree	10
8.)	Disagree	10
9.)	Agree	12
10.)	Disagree	10

Self-Rating Scale

280 and over	- Strong self-image; practically guilt free
255 to 279	- Relatively guilt free
230 to 254	- Only mild guilt
210 to 229	- About average
190 to 209	- Some weak areas
170 to 189	- Strong areas of guilt
150 to 169	- Easily manipulated
149 and below	- Very strong guilt feelings

INDEX